D0652145

Murder in the Carolinas

Murder in the Carolinas

by Nancy Rhyne

John F. Blair, Publisher
Winston-Salem, North Carolina

Copyright © 1988 by Nancy Rhyne
All rights reserved
Printed in the United States of America

Second Printing, 1988

Typesetting by Typography Studio,
    Winston-Salem, North Carolina
Printed by Edwards Brothers, Inc.

Library of Congress Cataloging-in-Publication Data

Rhyne, Nancy, 1926-
    Murder in the Carolinas.

    Bibliography: p.
    1. Murder—North Carolina—Case studies.   2. Murder
—South Carolina—Case studies.   I. Title.
HV6533.N8R48   1988   364.1'523'09756   88-19298
ISBN   0-89587-063-0

Contents

Acknowledgments

Each time I contemplate a new project, there are certain people I think of as excellent sources of information and assistance. When I actually start writing, I contact still others for their advice and knowledge. I can't begin to list everyone who assisted me in the collection and verification of facts for this book. But there are some whom I cannot fail to thank publicly, for without their help, this book would not have been written. I owe special thanks to the people I took by surprise when I stopped by their stores or homes in Pamplico. But there are others whose help in shaping the re-creation of the Bigham tale must be personally acknowledged. For her incomparable help, my deepest appreciation goes to Gladys Kirton Wingard of Lexington, South Carolina. I am also grateful to Blanche Floyd, Wynness Thomas, Mrs. W. A. Walker, and Florence Epps, who has been referred to as "Horry County's leading lady."

I am also indebted to Katie Snyder and Gladys Shuford of the Burke County Library in Morganton; Catherine H. Lewis, the county librarian for the Horry County libraries; Ann Dugger, the librarian in the Carolina Room of the Charlotte/Mecklenburg Library; Shirley Boone, Mary Owens, Linda Maher, Grace Kicidis, and Lesta Sue Hardee, all of the Chapin Memorial Library in Myrtle Beach; Elizabeth Whisnant of The State library in Columbia; Suzanne Singleton of the Sun News library in Myrtle Beach; Mrs. Tony Cimo and Mary and Howard Nestor of the Myrtle Beach area; Jack Leland of Charleston; Ralph McClendon of the Pottersville Museum in Edgefield; Mrs. Nancy Mims, author and archivist, of Edgefield; and last but not least, Margaret Couch and Carolyn Sakowski of John F. Blair, Publisher, who gave me the idea for this book and guided me through the undertaking.

My deepest appreciation also goes to my husband Sid for going along with me again, although he detested the very thought of pulling from the past such horrendous acts of crime.

Introduction

For those wondering why someone would write about men and women who have crossed the boundary of what we define as civilized behavior—by taking the life of another—I offer the reasons why frightful and horrid murder stories have always intrigued me.

It is true that I find grisly murder fascinating in a curious way. I want to satisfy my curiosity as to what has happened, and when and why and by whom. There must be a little bit of the detective in me, because I am drawn to crime stories, even if at a later time I sometimes wish I hadn't seen anything or heard anything about some of the cases.

When it comes down to it, who among us, at some time or other, hasn't grabbed an apple and a murder story and found a cozy corner in which to lose ourselves in an afternoon of intrigue? While reading a story of a spontaneous misdeed, or a crime of passion, we have to use our minds, figure out something. Our imaginations are rarely so challenged when we are reclining on a couch waiting to be entertained by a television program. And then there's that furtive element of a murder story that makes it fascinating only when we are safely away from the reality. It's akin to witnessing some sort of tragedy. We never want to happen upon an automobile accident, but when we do, we are left with an even keener regard for the sanctity of human life.

The stories that follow are true. They all took place in North or South Carolina during a span of almost two hundred years. However, my object as I sat at the typewriter was to tell a good tale, not merely give a step-by-step account of the facts. And some of the stories have been abbreviated because if I included all of the known facts, they would require a book unto themselves.

I invite you to grab an apple and find a cozy corner, and enjoy.

Murder in the Carolinas

A Devil of a Beauty

The story of Becky Cotton, a temptress and murderess if ever there was one, has fascinated people for nearly two centuries. In fact, the story has been so often repeated—from friend to friend, from historian to reader, from generation to generation—that fact is now inextricable from fiction.

One person is especially responsible for this co-mingling of fact and fiction. That man is Reverend Mason Locke Weems, not-so-affectionately referred to as "Parson Weems."

Parson Weems wrote several books and stories in a hellfire-and-damnation style, a fashion of his own that brought him criticism both from fellow authors and historians. A case in point is Weems's *Life of General Francis Marion*. After General Peter Horry of revolutionary war fame tried unsuccessfully to get the Library Society to publish his biography of Francis Marion, he turned to Weems. Weems could hardly wait to get his hands on the Marion manuscript. The Weems biography of Marion which appeared in 1809 was based on the work done by Peter Horry, but it was so embellished that Horry wrote Weems from Georgetown, South Carolina, on February 4, 1811, "Most certainly 'tis not my history, but your romance."

It was Parson Weems's belief that people wanted to be entertained while they were taught a moral lesson. Perhaps this explains the moralizing anecdote about George Washington chopping down the cherry tree, which is now attributed to Weems. It first appeared in the seventh edition of Weems's biography of Washington. Weems believed people would overlook almost anything so long as you amused them, and he was not above rearranging the facts if he could gain the interest of the readers. He also wasn't above avoiding an issue. When someone who was facing the hereafter with some trepidation asked Weems where he could expect to go after death, Weems cheerfully advised, "where all the other folks go."

The story of Becky Cotton, who became known as the "devil in petticoats," inspired Weems in the pulpit and at his writing desk. It's no longer possible to tell where Weems's embellishments for the sake of moral uplifting end and the unadulterated version begins. But no matter. The story of Becky Cotton won't disappoint anyone who loves a good murder tale.

Among Parson Weems's flock was one James Kannaday, the father of Becky Cotton. Of Kannaday, Parson Weems once wrote that there was little to his credit, although he would "for a pretence make long prayers." Old Kannaday was selfish and quarrelsome and many of his shameful quarrels ended in violence. But he also enjoyed the finer things in life, and he instilled in his daughter a taste for the type of life that he enjoyed. Kannaday lavished on her those things that he loved to gaze upon—beautiful clothes, silks, ribbons, and laces. Rebecca became strangely bewitched by these adornments and collected as many of them as she could charm out of her father—and later her many suitors. As time went on, she became more and more self-centered, just like her father.

Becky was a radiant beauty, and she used her stunning looks like a weapon—a poisonous Cupid's bow. Her suitors were legion. Finally, almost as a lark, she consented to marry one of the more ardent ones, Erasmus Smith.

The novelty of marriage did not disguise for long the fact that the match was a bad one. Smith was so besotted with Becky he could deny her nothing. Without any will of his own, he was no match for his wife. She dominated him and ordered his every movement. Still the young beauty wasn't satisfied, and she argued with him relentlessly. Smith's nerves suffered, and he soon was diminished to a pitiful state.

Becky was disgusted by her new husband; finally she could no longer even bear his touch. It wasn't long before it occurred to her that she didn't *have* to be trapped with this man for the rest of her life. "I'm beautiful and desirable. Why should my life be wasted?" she reasoned.

It was never clear whether Becky plotted her husband's demise or if she acted spontaneously when she saw her opportunity. But one night, as her husband dozed in his armchair by the fire, Becky seized a mattress needle and stabbed him through the heart. Smith was of slight stature, but still it took all of Becky's strength to drag the body through the woods and down to nearby Beaverdam Creek. With the last of her strength, she weighed the body down with chains and rolled it into the black, swampy water.

Neighbors knew that Becky's marriage was a failure, so they weren't surprised when she told them Smith had run off and abandoned her. Sympathy was offered in abundance: "The poor creature. So young and lovely to bear such a disappointment." Weeks later, when Becky tearfully spread the news she had received word that her husband was dead, most of her acquaintances whispered it was for the best.

Hardly a year had passed since the disappearance of her first husband before Becky accepted the proposal of her second. Joshua Terry was just as bewitched by her good looks as his luckless predecessor had been. He rhapsodized about her silken hair, her ivory skin, her delicate form.

But his joy didn't even last through the honeymoon. Evidently Becky wasn't afraid to reveal her true nature as soon as the marriage vows were taken. She tormented her second husband just as she had the first, but Joshua Terry clung to the dream of a happy life with Becky with unbelievable tenacity. Regardless of how cruelly she berated him, Terry took no action against her.

He was still madly in love with Becky when she killed him one snowy December night. She administered a deadly potion of nightshade to him in place of his asthma medicine. The wind was howling as Becky dragged Terry's body down to the deep waters of the creek to join the body of her first husband.

There was no question that in 1800 Becky was still a ravishing beauty. Undaunted by the strange disappearance of two husbands, suitors flocked to her door. It was at that time that she caught the attention of a man named Cotton. She would always call him Cotton—before and after they were married.

Cotton was a hard-working man who had acquired ownership of some acreage and a one-room house with a loft. Cotton knew Becky had an explosive temper, but he was convinced he was the one to effect the "taming of the shrew." And for a while, he thought he had succeeded. When they were first married, he liked nothing more than working hard and spending his profits on exquisite linens and laces for Becky; and that suited Becky just fine. Perhaps Becky was afraid the fates of her first two husbands would be discovered, but she seemed to calm down and make an effort to live with Cotton.

Years passed and Becky bore Cotton two children, a son and a daughter. Unlike many women of her time, childbearing only increased Becky's beauty. But she was also growing restless. When she finally decided that Cotton did not possess the disposition that she desired in a lifelong mate, Cotton did not even notice her disenchantment. He was too blinded by his love for Becky to notice her increasingly selfish and demanding ways.

Cotton was also anxious and uneasy because he feared the violence that was rampant in their area. And Cotton's fear of the unruly people of Edgefield County was not unfounded. So many murders were committed there that when word of another was spread, people were inclined to cry, "Oh mercy! Old Edgefield again. Another murder in Edgefield!"

Becky became so exasperated with Cotton's apprehensions that she finally invited her young brother Davis to move in with them. Fourteen-year-old Davis was a person whom she could manipulate, and besides that, she enjoyed having him around to wait on her.

Throughout the years, Becky remained devoted to one person— her father. James Kannaday was a frequent visitor at the Cotton home. One day Kannaday met some of his angered neighbors in a corn field. Kannaday's corn field adjoined one of his neighbor's, and Kannaday was accused of allowing his horses and hogs to feed on the corn beyond the property line. In that neighborhood, allowing your livestock to cross a property line into a neighbor's field was tantamount to a declaration of war. A terrible fight ensued, and Kannaday ran away, shamelessly beaten.

Becky and Cotton were sitting in the house when Kannaday burst in on them. Behind him came an angry mob who pushed their way into the cabin. Becky's children were in the loft and Davis was away.

"What is it?" Becky screamed to her father.

"It's their confounded corn," Kannaday mumbled. "They said my horses and hogs went across the line to feed."

Becky turned to Cotton for support, but he was pale and trembling. Becky stared at Cotton, her disdain for this weak man deepening with every second. It was finally left to Becky to go out on the porch and chase away the mob.

Days later, as soon as Kannaday had recovered from the beating, he set out for Charleston. The roads leading to Charleston were dangerous for the wayfarer. Frequently, men would hide under the tents of covered wagons and ambush travelers, whipping them and stealing anything of value from the mangled bodies. But Kannaday made it safely to Charleston, where he took out a number of bench warrants against his assailants. After returning home, he joyously announced that he had been a match for the rascals. He went to Becky's house to share the news with her.

When the gang heard what Kannaday had done, they were outraged. They loaded their guns, mounted their horses, and headed for Kannaday's home. Not finding him there, they headed for the Cotton household. When they stormed the house, Kannaday just turned pale and trembled like a frightened child. Cotton, too, was petrified with terror and completely helpless.

All of the hate and disgust in Becky's heart emerged as she rushed toward the mean-tempered men, her face flushed with rage. She screamed at them, wanting to know how they dared threaten a gentleman in his own house. Suddenly recognizing that murder was their intent, Becky threw herself on her father and cried that if they murdered him they would murder her also. For some moments, the assassins stood at bay, but just as Becky turned for an instant, one of them placed the muzzle of his gun to the old man's side and shot him through the heart in order "to send the old hypocrite to hell at once!"

After the burial, Becky and Cotton had a terrible argument.

"You knew very well," she yelled, "when you saw those villains standing there that they were going to murder my poor father, for they were swearing it on every breath. You had only to snatch up your gun and point it at them, and they would have regretted that they dared to darken your door!"

Cotton hadn't come to the defense of Becky's father, and feeling that her husband should have been brave enough to hold off the hoodlums, Becky lost any love that she had for Cotton. From that time forth her intentions toward him became as sinister and wicked as those she had displayed against his predecessors.

A great coldness developed in the family, and the love that Cotton had felt for Becky also turned to hate. Becky moved to the loft, where her children and her brother slept. Each day when Cotton came home from the fields, his wife was nowhere to be seen, and no food was on the table. The children became as irritable as their parents.

It occurred to Cotton that it wasn't out of the question for Becky to murder him. Murder was almost epidemic all around them in Edgefield County, and Becky had been a devil since the death of her father. He sensed that she itched to retaliate against him. And he started to wonder about the mysterious disappearances of her two previous husbands.

One day when a friend stopped by the field and invited Cotton to come to his house for supper, Cotton gladly accepted the invitation. The idea of a good home-cooked meal sounded enticing. It was a pleasant time of relaxed conversation and delicious food. As Cotton took his leave, he thought of the future and shook his head.

"What is it?" his host asked.

Cotton regarded his friend blindly and said, "If I knew that the road to my house was beset by Indians, I could hardly set out home with more uneasiness than I now do, for I am very sure that I shall be murdered shortly." His intuition was on target, for at that very moment Becky was awaiting his return. She had deemed that night in 1803 to be Cotton's last.

The first person Cotton saw when he returned home was Becky's brother. "Where's your sister?"

"She has gone to bed."

"Is she sick?"

"Yes."

Cotton sat by the fire for a while pondering his fate. Finally, in deep despair, he trudged off to bed. Before long he was breathing steadily and drifting off to sleep.

Becky quietly climbed down the ladder. Light from a full moon flooded the room and gave everything a ghostly look. Her ears picked up the sound of Cotton's steady breathing. She was glad he hadn't noticed that she had taken the axe from the woodpile and concealed it under a towel in a corner of the room. Becky quietly stepped to the corner and removed the towel. She picked up the axe and walked toward the bed. Cotton hadn't moved since she had come down the ladder.

For a moment Becky observed the figure lying before her. He was a weakling, she thought. Why had she ever married him in the first place? If he had any nerve her father would be living tonight. She couldn't put up with him any longer.

Becky lifted the axe and brought it down hard on Cotton's head. There was a moan as the blade struck his skull and some slight movement of his legs, then all was still. Becky hurried up the ladder and called for her brother. Poor Davis was too scared to do anything but pull on his clothes and climb down to help her as she demanded. They buried the corpse in a potato vault behind the house.

If Becky Cotton had a quality to match the wickedness that had flowered in her years before, it was her cunning. To explain Cotton's disappearance, there would have to be a reason for him to flee the country. As she thought about it, something came to her. She vaguely remembered it, but some months before a man had come to their door and accused Cotton of stealing some bags from his cart. While Becky was listening to the conversation, she had thought disdainfully that Cotton wouldn't have the nerve even to take a measly bag of goods. But now, she could go to the authorities and claim that Cotton had indeed taken the bags from the wagoner's cart. At the time of the accusation, it was so ridiculous that Becky had dismissed it from her mind. But now it could become the tool she needed. If her dead husband had made any other enemy in the world, she probably could have come up with a more plausible story, but Cotton had no foes. Besides, experience led her to believe she didn't need a better story.

The next day Becky went to the authorities and told them that her husband and a strange wagoner had recently had a terrible quarrel about some bags. "Cotton stole the wagoner's bags and has run off to escape justice."

During the days that followed, the neighbors grew increasingly suspicious. Cotton had told many of them that he and Becky fought like cats and dogs. He had even anticipated his murder. Curiously, they didn't begin speculating on the disappearances of Becky's first two husbands. As the people in the neighborhood talked about it, they came to the conclusion that Becky might have killed Cotton, but she would have needed help in order to dispose of the two-hundred-pound body. There was only one person who would have been willing to help with such a heinous deed: her brother, Davis.

The suspicion that Becky had murdered her husband escalated. One neighbor even went from house to house giving a long discourse on the probable course of events. Many believed every word. Even the church wardens and law officers were now convinced that Becky had taken Cotton's life. The officers decided to set a trap. They knew that Becky was too smart not to suspect treachery, but Davis was of another nature. Surely he had helped Becky, or at least he would know something of the crime. They believed they could trick him.

Davis was walking in a remote area when he was grabbed and taken to the home of a man who lived in the community. Neighbors of the Cottons were sent for, and Davis was threatened with torture unless he told the truth. Fearing their threat was sincere, he admitted that Becky had killed Cotton and buried him in the potato vault. The men flew to the spot and found the corpse. Then they began to look for Becky. They searched the house, including the loft, the barn, and all the out buildings, but she wasn't there. Where was Becky, they wondered, and what had she done with the children? Davis would know!

Again under threat, Davis admitted that the children had been sent to relatives and Becky was on her way out West. A law enforcement officer was sent in pursuit of the murderess. Within a week Becky was found. She was brought home and charged with the murder of her husband.

On the day of Becky Cotton's trial, the courtroom was filled to capacity. Every neck was craned toward the door in anticipation of her arrival. Finally, she appeared.

Becky, looking tragic and sweetly vulnerable in her widow's weeds, entered the courtroom as though walking to music. She sashayed near the judge's bench and sat down. When she was called to testify, she kissed the Bible and glided to the witness chair. In a lyrical voice, she spoke of the innocent life she had led, how she had cared for members of her family, especially her brother, Davis. As she spoke of her father's death, she removed a handkerchief of lace from a pocket and touched the corners of her eyes. Oh so strange and hard to believe, she said, that both her father and husband died at the hands of murderers. Her delicate beauty and girlish voice captivated the all-male jury.

The jury deliberated. Davis had not testified; he was thought to be too young and unreliable to give evidence in a capital case. There were no other eyewitnesses. Becky never confessed, tearfully maintaining that someone else had killed Cotton. The men discussed all this. Finally, they were ushered back into the courtroom.

There was a hush. The verdict was announced. Becky Cotton was acquitted. She waltzed out of the courtroom a free woman.

"Oh, heavens, what a charming creature," a man whispered.

"Yes," replied his companion, "if she had not been such a murderer."

"A murderer?" one of the jury members debated angrily. "A murderer, sir, 'tis false! Such an angel could never have been a murderer."

Among the members of the jury who had been taken in by Becky's charms was Major Ellis, a widower from Edgefield who owned considerable property. Major Ellis noted Becky's grace as she stood at the bar of justice and the lovely, soft hands that moved so slightly as she spoke. He refused to believe that those very hands had recently held a murder weapon—an axe!—it wasn't possible. Soon after the trial, Major Ellis called upon Becky and asked her hand in marriage. She accepted.

"Oh, Major Ellis," a friend exclaimed, "how could you marry a murderess? What would your wife, that excellent lady now lying in the grave, think?"

"She is asleep. One doesn't think when one sleeps," he answered sardonically.

Although married to Major Ellis, she remained Becky Cotton to most of her neighbors and was seldom referred to as Mrs. Ellis. As soon as she settled into the Ellis home, which was far more comfortable than any she had known, she began to pull strings to get her brother, Stephen Kannaday, into the household, just as she had once arranged for Davis to live with her. With no regard for scruples or conscience, Becky advised Stephen that she thought it would be to his advantage to attract the major's eldest daughter.

"You will notice her beauty, especially for a person of thirteen years," Becky remarked to Stephen, "but I am obliged to inform you that she possesses a pretty fortune." Becky went on to tutor Stephen in how to attract the young woman, and she said that if a marriage between the two took place, she would persuade Major Ellis to settle on Stephen the property intended for the daughter.

"I have tied myself to bed and board for life with the one you chose for me," Stephen said to Becky after the marriage ceremony. "Fulfill your promise to me. I want the property that the major reserved for my wife."

Becky answered that she had every intention of advising her husband to make a change in the title to the land, but it would take time. However, the more she thought about it, the more she decided that she would keep all the assets for herself. She neglected to tell Stephen of her change in plans.

Although she was pleased that Stephen had married the girl, it was also her wish that they live on another plantation and not underfoot. Becky's poise was going to suffer a real blow if Stephen didn't back off a little on the property title change. The situation was becoming more difficult all the time, but Becky was now beginning to think of *her* future. If her husband should die, then he would leave everything to her. But if Stephen obtained title to a tract of land, there would be no way she as a widow could regain title to the property. But Becky did need to talk to Stephen. She needed him to do her one more favor.

The major owed a friend two hundred and fifty dollars, and the friend was holding the note. Stephen would have to get his hands on that document. If he brought the note to her, Becky promised, Stephen could have the full-time use of a valuable family servant. When Stephen was successful in the mission and handed the note to Becky, she again failed to make good on her promise.

"This is beyond all bearing," Stephen snarled.

"You're no match for me, Stephen," Becky answered. "Haven't you figured out that your harshest words are of no consequence to me? What can you possibly do to hurt me?"

"If your wicked doings don't carry you to hell, then there's no use for the place," Stephen snapped. "You're as dishonest as the day is long!"

"If you play the fool with me," Becky said, getting riled up, "you will awaken in hellfire much sooner than you wish!"

Stephen thought about that remark. He knew that Becky had murdered before, and she could do so again. The more he thought about it, the more alarmed he became.

Several months later a farm hand told Stephen that Becky was carrying two armed pistols with her at all times. "She plans to kill you," the man warned. Stephen became more and more nervous, reduced to a deplorable condition that continued to worsen until spring.

One day in May 1807 Becky called for her carriage. She took the reins herself and drove to the courthouse. As she stepped from the coach a man standing nearby came over to talk. Just then Stephen happened to walk by them. He was pale and thin; his physical condition had deteriorated due to his worry that he would be Becky's next victim. In his mind, it was not only likely that he would be her next casualty, it was simply a matter of when it would happen.

"You have ruined my life," Stephen shouted irrationally.

"What under the sun do you mean?" Becky questioned. She glanced quizzically at her acquaintance, in an effort to dispel any suspicion that she knew what Stephen was shouting about in such a virulent tone.

"You know what I mean," Stephen barked. "You're planning to kill me, and my senses have been so abused that I remain in my house most of the time lest I be shot in the head."

"Oh, he's out of his mind," Becky sighed. "I can't imagine why he's carrying on so."

"You have loaded pistols in your skirts right now," Stephen screamed.

"But, sir," the bystander interjected, "your sister is a charming woman, and a lady of singular beauty. Surely she could not be guilty of your charges."

Stephen ignored the man. "By God, *I'll* kill *you*, Becky!" he ranted. Suddenly he stopped, looking stunned, as though he had just then thought about such a thing. "Yes, I'll kill you." Amid a violent eruption of tears, he stooped for a rock and struck it against Becky's head. She fell, but he kept hitting her forehead with the stone, over and over, and those standing nearby were in such a stupor they did not restrain him. Finally Stephen stood, Becky crumpled at his feet. He kicked her with his boot, then turned and went to a fence where he untied his horse. Stephen galloped away, leaving Becky Cotton lying dead in front of the courthouse. He took his wife and they ran away somewhere out West, never returning.

Death had come at last to "the devil in petticoats."

Poetry on the Gallows

The wind was blowing so hard it fairly shook our cabin. And it was keening a mournful sound. You know I thought it could have been the song of my heart. I was so sad it weighed on me so I could hardly move, or think. Then I heard a bobcat screech outside, and for some reason that set me to moving.

I took Nancy and laid her in her cradle. My Charlie had fallen asleep on the hearth with her in his arms. He looked like a little boy alayin' there and, Lord, he was so handsome my heart nearly stopped. But I played out my plan and slipped out to the woodpile and got the axe.

When I stepped back inside, I remember it seemed so hot. I suppose it just seemed so comin' in from the cold. Anyway, I walked over to Charlie and hefted the axe and brought it right down on his neck. Blood spurted all over the room from that big vein in the neck. But, Lord, he wasn't dead yet and he half raised up and moaned and I brought the axe down again just as quick as I could to keep from hearing his cries and him from suffering. The second strike hit him in the back. That one did it.

Frankie stopped her narrative, lost in thought. She was staring at the far wall, eyes unseeing. Her friend Clara watched her closely. Frankie no longer acted or looked like the pretty young girl with laughing eyes Clara loved so well. She was pale, with deep circles under her eyes. And there was something gone from her. Hope, perhaps.

"But why, Frankie, *why* did you do it?" Clara asked, gently but urgently.

After a moment, Frankie took up her story as if she hadn't even heard her friend's question.

Oh, Clara. I was happy, so very happy at first. Charlie was kind, so full of fun. He was a favorite at all the parties and, oh, how I loved to hear him play his fife.

I wasn't raised in the mountains, you know, but in the lowlands, in Anson County. Charlie was a mountain man, though, and I didn't mind moving to Deyton's Bend. I didn't even mind the cabin—though it was only one room. I didn't mind anything as long as Charlie Silver loved me.

And he did love me then, I'm sure of it. He went on and on about my fair skin and my bright eyes, and he sure was impressed that I could card and spin three yards of cotton a day.

The cabin is in the shadow of Mount Mitchell, and the place is wild. But I felt adorned by the heavens and haloed by the stars. . . . I put that in one of my poems. Did you ever read that one?

Frankie didn't pause for an answer. She was talking to herself as much as to Clara.

Last summer—no it's been two summers now—I used to walk along the banks of the Toe River when the rhododendron and mountain laurel were in bloom. Oh, the mountains are harsh, but they are mighty beautiful. But the winters, they're different. It wasn't long before I learned the mountains during winter are as cold as death. The night blasts of cold turn them into marble.

I was awful lonesome that winter. My nearest neighbors were miles away, and mountain miles are toilsome distances. Folks didn't visit around much between November and March up there.

I never complained about the loneliness, or the cold, or anything else, until after our daughter Nancy was born. Charlie changed, became bent on pleasure. I'd always thought he was *my* man, but he began to spend days—then nights—away from home. Many nights I would lay awake and listen for his footsteps on the frozen ground, but they didn't come. The moon would climb high in the sky, and then wane, but Charlie didn't come home. During those long nights, I began to wonder if my man was in the arms of another woman.

I didn't really believe it, not at first. One day he came home at dawn. Been out all night. I said, 'Charlie, where have you been? I've been worried near half to death.' He just slammed his fist against the wall and said, 'Woman, mind your own damn business!' Then he grabbed one of my poems—it was layin' on the mantel—and wadded it up and threw it into the flames.

He came home drunker'n a pole cat in a barrel of whiskey a few days later. I said, 'Charlie, I need you at home. I need you sober.' He hit me, Clara. He hit me again and again.

I thought my heart would break clean in two, but I spent my time tending to Nancy and tried to get through the days. Then I heard some talk 'bout Charlie and Zeb Cranberry's wife. I'd had enough of skulking about the cabin, afraid to do something that would set him to hittin' me. So I asked him right out about the gossip. . . . He beat me near senseless.

I never asked him where he spent his time again. I never showed my jealousy or hurt again. But the drinking and the beatings, they got worse. And they took their toll on my soul.

Clara interrupted. "But why didn't you tell your dad or your brothers? I know Isaiah Stewart and he would've done something to protect his daughter. And what of Blackstone?"

Yes. They likely would have killed him. My daddy sets great store by me. And Blackstone's a bull. He could've torn Charlie limb from limb. But I was ashamed and, besides, you know I'm most general not one for talking about private things. I had to settle it myself.

I planned how I would do it. I thought about it for weeks. Charlie often fell asleep by the fire. And I'd chopped wood before—I could handle an axe.

Charlie told me that morning—I mean the day I killed him, December 22, 1831—he told me he was leaving for a few days to go hunting. But he didn't prepare for a hunt like he usually did. I knew he was going off for a tryst with some woman. Maybe Mrs. Cranberry. So I knew that was the night.

I said, 'Charlie, chop as much wood as you can before you leave.' The snow was deep and the woodpile was low so he had to know I really did need wood. He went out and chopped a big stack. But I saw it wouldn't be enough. I'd need more. So I said, 'Cut more.' He did. And after I chopped his body up, I used that wood to burn the pieces.

Clara gasped. She had heard the story, of course, but she still was shocked at Frankie's matter-of-fact account. Frankie kept on, oblivious to Clara.

I worked frantically. It was straining work . . . harder than I thought to cut the body up into small enough pieces. And the blood kept spewing onto the mantel. But I couldn't worry about that yet. The fire was dying down. The blood, I guess. I continually ran outside and brought in great arm loads of wood to keep the fire going.

Finally, it was almost done. I took some of his larger bones and joints that I was afraid wouldn't burn, and his heart—I couldn't bear to toss that into the fire—and took them out and buried them in a hollow stump. . . . A dog found them, you know, when the spring thaw came. But I was already in jail by then.

Anyway, when I went back to the cabin, I scrubbed the floor and whittled away the bloodstains on the mantel. The dawn was breaking by then, and I was plumb shakin' with exhaustion. Nancy woke up, and I fed her. Then I went back to work. My clothes still had to be washed free of blood.

I was so tired, but I wasn't through yet. I still had to go visit Charlie's family as if nothing had happened. I bundled Nancy up and walked all the way over the frozen snow. The women were washing clothes. I was nervous, and I remember Charlie's mama said to me, 'You can't keep still, girl. What's wrong with you?'

I had to go back to his family again later that day to report Charlie didn't come home when I was expectin' him. I said, 'Charlie went to fetch whiskey for Christmas. He hasn't come home. Perhaps he fell in the river.'

It was just two days until Christmas. Several people came by askin' about Charlie, and I told them all the same story about him being out after whiskey. But Jake Collis, I could tell he didn't believe me.

By the day after Christmas, Charlie's father John was desperate with worry. John's a good enough man. I felt sorry for him—he was at his wit's end. Been out looking for his son everywhere. He says to me, 'Frankie, I'm agoin' to see Silas Williams's old Guinea Negro. Maybe he can look in his magic glass and see where Charlie is.' John walked forty miles to Silas's farm in Tennessee. Lord, I was scared to death that old Negro really might be able to see Charlie, what was left of him.

But John hadn't even come back yet before I was discovered.

Frankie sat silent, staring into her own private hell. Clara knew Frankie had a stoic personality, but she knew her friend wasn't as imperturbable as she seemed. The silence stretched into minutes. "Do you want to go on?" she asked.

Yes. My hanging is in four days. I want someone finally to know *my* story. Someday maybe my little Nancy will need to hear it.

Well, Jake Collis, like I said, was suspicious. He came and searched the cabin, just like he owned the place. I reckon some of the bones and teeth didn't burn 'cause he found them in the fireplace. And the ashes were greasy, too, he said. He looked at the mantel, you know, where I had chipped away the bloodstains. He looked at the stains on the floor. I scrubbed and scrubbed, but it still looked a sight.

Jake left, but I knew the murder was discovered. He came back later with some other men. I just stood aside, holding Nancy, and let them do their lookin'.

About that time John Silver threw open the cabin door. He was just back from Tennessee and had heard the news. I could see it on his face. He just looked at me, disbelieving like, and said, 'Frankie. Frankie.'

Then John, he told the other men how the magic glass had been right after all. The old conjurer wasn't at the farm, but Silas Williams read the glass. John said, 'The glass turned downward, and Silas claimed that meant Charlie would be found at home. I thought I had walked forty miles for naught.'

The law came next. The sheriff and his man looked all around, and they asked me questions. But I never told anyone what I had done. I just played dumb. I was arrested on the tenth day of January. Little Nancy was taken right out of my arms. She was wailing, but I was crying silent tears. They brought me to the jail here, in Morganton.

Did you hear they arrested my mama and Blackstone, too? I reckon they couldn't believe I'd done such a deed by myself. But daddy raised Cain and got a habeas corpus writ. There was some kind of proceedings. I wasn't there. But my mama and brother were released.

My trial started at the end of March. It only lasted two days. You were there. My lawyer pleaded me not guilty. Mama thought I shoulda pleaded self-defense. The judge, John Donnell, he seemed like a fair man.

You know, when the doctor testified that the pieces of bone they found in the stump were human bones and that the heart was a human heart, it chilled my very soul. I mean I knew I had done the murder. But the whole time while I was hefting the axe and then chopping up Charlie's body, it was like I was standin' outside of myself. Like I was awatchin' some other woman who was me doing all those things.

Again, Frankie stopped. She got up and started to pace the cell.

Then, still moving back and forth in a regular rhythm, she continued her narrative.

The best thing about the trial was getting to hold my baby on my lap through it all. But then it ended. On the thirtieth of March the jury came in, and they said I was guilty. They looked uncomfortable, like they wished it wasn't so. I reckon that's 'cause I'm a woman. The sheriff told me I'd be the first white woman ever to be hanged in North Carolina.

Anyway, the decree, it said Frankie Silver should be 'hung by the neck until she be dead on the Friday of July court next of Burke County.' I'll never forget those words.

My lawyer and my folks insisted on an appeal. But the verdict, it was upheld.

They told me a new execution date would be set at the next superior court session in September 1832. The judge—Swain, he's the governor now—didn't show up for the court. I didn't know whether to be grateful or not. I was in jail nine months by then, and the time was wearing on me heavy.

But I didn't have any say so in any of this, and they didn't set a new hanging date until March, a full year from my trial. The new execution date was June 28, 1833.

"Why'd you try to escape, Frankie?" Clara asked. "You oughta knowed they'd hunt you down like a scared rabbit."

I wasn't thinking about getting caught. I was thinking about that rope around my neck, snapping it like it was no more'n a dry twig. And I was thinking of Nancy. What was to become of her? It wasn't fair for her to lose her papa *and* her mama before she was yet two years old.

Besides, Daddy and my uncle and my brothers were awful anxious to try the escape. They couldn't hardly stand to see me cooped up like an animal. And the thought of me ahangin' on the gallows, well, they were terrible insistent on the escape. I just didn't argue.

So on the eighteenth of June, just ten days before the hanging was to be, my daddy and uncle entered the jail through a window in the basement. Somehow they had a set of keys, and they just came right in and got me. We left through the same window. Didn't get far, though, just to Rutherford County. I cut my hair short and they had men's clothes for me to dress in, but the disguise didn't keep the sheriff from finding us.

When they brought me back to the Morganton jail, I found out the day of execution had been changed again—to the twelfth of July. Fourteen more days added. I still don't know why. . . . The sheriff says Governor Swain may have granted a stay of execution.

Frankie sat down, her agitation suddenly gone. The day was waning, and the sunlight had moved across the cell walls and was fading away.

That's my story, Clara, or most of it. I'm setting something down on this paper here to read at the hanging. Please help mama take care of Nancy if you can.

A huge crowd was gathered on Damon's Hill the day of the hanging. Some had even climbed trees in order to get a better view. It seemed that all of the mountain people wanted to see Frankie Silver go to her reward. Frankie climbed onto the scaffold with the help of Sheriff John Boone.

As the noose was placed about her neck, Frankie whispered to the hangman that she would like to say a few words before she died. It was her last wish, and the request was granted. In a clear and calm voice, Frankie recited the poem she had written for the occasion of her hanging.

> This dreadful, dark and dismal day
> Has swept my glories all away—
> My sun goes down, my days are past,
> And I must leave this world at last.
>
> Oh! Lord, what will become of me?
> I am condemned you all now see
> To heaven or hell my soul must fly,
> All in a moment when I die.
>
> Judge Donnell has my sentence pass'd
> These prison walls I leave at last.
> Nothing to cheer my drooping head
> Until I'm numbered with the dead.
>
> But oh! That dreadful Judge I fear,
> Shall I that awful sentence hear?
> "Depart ye cursed down to hell
> And forever there to dwell."

I know that frightful ghosts I'll see
Gnawing their flesh in misery,
And then and there attended be
For murder in the first degree.

There shall I meet that mournful face
Whose blood I spilled upon this place;
With flaming eyes to me he'll say:
"Why did you take my life away?"

His feeble hands fell gently down,
His chattering tongue soon lost its sound
To see his soul and body part
It strikes with terror to my heart.

I took his blooming days away,
Left him no time to God to pray,
And if sins fall on his head
Must I not bear them in his stead?

The jealous thought that first gave strife
To make me take my husband's life,
For months and days I spent my time
Thinking how to commit this crime.

And on a dark and doleful night
I put his body out of sight,
With flames I tried him to consume
But time would not admit it done.

You all see me and on me gaze,
Be careful how you spend your days,
And never commit this awful crime,
But try to serve your God in time.

My mind on solemn subjects roll;
My little child, God bless its soul!
All you that are of Adam's race,
Let not my faults this child disgrace.

Farewell good people, you all now see
What my bad conduct's brought on me—
To die of shame and of disgrace
Before this world of human race.

Awful indeed to think of death,
In perfect health to lose my breath,
Farewell my friends, I bid adieu,
Vengeance on me must not pursue.

Great God! How shall I be forgiven?
Not fit for earth, not fit for heaven,
But for little time to pray to God,
For now I try that awful road.

Throughout the trial, the love that Frankie Silver's family felt for her never swayed. After the hanging, while Sheriff John Boone received the statutory fee of ten dollars, her brothers claimed the body. It was lovingly lowered into the coffin, which was then placed on a wagon. Blackstone swung up the reins, called to the horse, and off they went, bearing the corpse of Frankie Silver. The day was stiflingly hot, and the Stewarts began to talk of their superstitious fears relating to the decomposition of a body on such a hot day. Taking that into consideration, they abandoned their plan of taking Frankie's body home to Deyton's Bend for burial, and she was laid to rest on the farm of Jake Devault on Yellow Mountain Road, eight miles from Morganton.

Frankie's tragic poem was put to music and frequently sung in the mountains. Several of the melodies have survived. The poem has been remarkably well preserved by oral tradition—all of the versions are almost identical. Even today, it's not surprising to hear Frankie's mournful story sung at gatherings in the mountains.

The Woman Who Was Murdered Twice

"Are you truly Polly Middleton?" asked the woman who had just opened the door.

"Yes, I'm Polly," the pathetic-looking girl standing on the wraparound porch answered timidly. No one in the world had experienced more ups and downs than Polly, except most of Polly's experiences were downs. However, at this very moment, it seemed so good to be back at her lovely childhood home that Polly's eyes were luminous and sparkling.

"Well, come in, my dear. I've long wanted to meet you."

Hugging her baby to her chest, Polly glided through the door into the adjoining drawing room. It's a success so far, she was thinking, although she knew if her father came in and laid eyes on her and her illegitimate child he might throw them out without so much as a fare-thee-well. But she saw no indication that he was about, and the atmosphere was relaxed and friendly, almost jovial. Mrs. Middleton appeared to be at ease, for the moment at least. Polly sat down on the sofa, beside her hostess.

"Polly," Mrs. Middleton said a little hesitantly, "my husband, uh, your father, is away, but I expect him at any time."

Polly's heart did a flip-flop. It would be just like her father to abuse her. He had been no father to her since her mother had died so many years ago. He hated her so much because of the child that he might even kill her in a moment of rage. Still, she was out of options.

"As you know," Mrs. Middleton continued, "your father is dogged and relentless, and I must tell you that he doesn't look kindly upon your life. That is, uh, the child."

Polly's heart beat even more rapidly as she clutched her baby tighter. "Do you think he'll throw us out?"

Mrs. Middleton shifted nervously in her chair, a bit flustered by the directness of Polly's question. "I cannot answer that, but let us go upstairs where you will be comfortable for the time being." She led the way to the staircase, wondering if Polly had eaten lately. She looked half-starved. "Have you eaten today?"

After a short silence, Polly answered, "No. Not today."

Mrs. Middleton immediately summoned a servant to fix a meal and bring it upstairs. "One of the servants will attend to the baby," she added. "Is it a boy?"

"Yes," Polly answered, fierce pride rising in her. "His name is Billy."

In the bedroom, Polly looked around, her eyes darting from side to side with unconcealed curiosity—and sadness. This had been her mother's room. It looked much the same. A lump came to Polly's throat, and she shuddered. My dear mother, stricken by death so early in life! By now a servant was taking the little boy, and Mrs. Middleton was saying something about eating the food set before her. But Polly was lost in her thoughts. Mrs. Middleton quietly left the room, and her guest laid down on the high, four-poster bed and allowed old memories to surge through her mind.

It was on this very bed that Polly had been born, and here her mother had died of consumption. The first grief Polly had ever known came to her on the day of her mother's death in 1801, for her life until that time had been a charmed one as a daughter of the Hugh Middletons, who lived on a plantation in the district of Edgefield. In her last moments, Polly's mother had murmured, "Oh, my God, what will become of my poor children when I am gone?" At the time five-year-old Polly, too, had wondered what would become of her.

Major Middleton hadn't remained a widower for very long, but his second wife reserved her love for others. She was not the loving stepmother the three young girls so desperately needed. At her best moments, she was indifferent to them. At her worst, she was cruel. In fact, there was never a glow of tender sentiment in the woman at all until her own children were born. After that time, Polly and her two sisters were not allowed to sleep in beds, but instead were consigned to the kitchen hearth.

Before her mother died, Polly's father had called her his "own little angel." There had been so much love in the Middleton house then, and Polly grieved for what she had lost. Never again would anyone love her, she feared. Her mother had now turned to dust, and her father was indifferent to her. Although it was a painful and crushing situation for Polly, and she detested her life, she was too young and powerless to change her circumstances.

Years passed, and the oldest of Polly's sisters married at an early age. Polly pleaded to live with her. Knowing what life was like at the Middleton plantation, her sister couldn't deny Polly's entreaty. It wasn't the best of arrangements, but Polly tried to comfort her troubled mind with memories of her mother.

One day word came to the household that Polly's stepmother was dead and her father had taken a new wife. Perhaps his new wife was as bad-tempered as the last. But perhaps not. It might be worth a try to go home and see if there would be a little room and love for her in the big house with the wraparound porch.

Polly was working on her stitchery, daydreaming about going back to her father's home, when her sister surprised her with the news a relative of her husband's was coming to live with them. After all, her sister pointed out, they had taken in one of *her* relatives when Polly moved in last year. She would now return the kindness and take in one of her husband's kin.

The next day, Polly carefully observed the young man as he was moving into the room upstairs. As she plied perfect stitches, her eyes caught glimpses of a dark-haired man of obvious strength. When he saw Polly eyeing him, he smiled a most kindly smile. Polly bit her lip nervously. Her eyes dropped as she sucked in her breath and clenched the piece of linen in her lap. The smile had all but paralyzed her.

"You must be Polly," the man said.

"I am," she answered, her heart beating a little less frenziedly.

"Pleased to be meetin' you," he said. His grin was impish and his eyes twinkling. "My name's Jack."

He is so full of cheer and joy, Polly thought. She cleared her throat and swallowed deeply. Maybe she wouldn't go to her father's house quite yet.

To Jack, Polly looked godforsaken and lonely. She seemed a lifeless child in one way, yet there was a vibrancy lurking somewhere in her depths. A knot twisted in his stomach.

At first Jack was like a brother to Polly, sincere and caring. She was all innocence as she enjoyed the first bonds of love and friendship and sympathy she had known since her mother's death. Jack exuded everything that Polly had once loved but lost. He was lively and witty and intelligent. There was a lighthearted self-confidence in him. Oh! It's wonderful to have Jack here, she thought.

Some weeks passed, and Polly relished the closeness of Jack. She was comfortable with her life for the first time in many years. One evening Polly asked Jack to close a window because she was chilled by the wind. He removed the stick and eased the window down, then went to the sofa and put his arms around Polly to warm her. She moved slightly within his arms, and when he kissed her she realized she had not been kissed by anyone since her mother kissed her on her death bed. Polly returned all the love offered her, and within months she learned that she was expecting Jack's child.

When her pregnancy was discovered, her sister unceremoniously threw Polly out of the house. She fled, not telling anyone where she was going. After a few days of wandering, she found a family who took her in, and she remained with them until after her son was born, when she decided to continue her original plan to go see her father. As she had wondered more than a year before, she again contemplated what her stepmother might be like. And what of her father? It had been a long time since they had seen each other. Would he turn her away because of the illegitimate child? Or would he remember his "own little angel"?

Now that she was in her father's house, her questions were still unanswered. Suddenly Polly's reverie was shattered by a thundering voice, black with rage. It was her father, coming upstairs, where she was resting. He stopped in the doorway. Polly now saw with unmistakable clarity the renunciation on his face, the repudiation in his eyes.

"Stain of my family! Detested wretch! Begone!" he howled.

Polly just stared at her father, beyond tears and beyond hope.

Mrs. Middleton called from the stairs. "But poor Polly has come with her little child to implore your forgiveness."

"What! Forgive a wretch who has disgraced my name and scandalized my family? No! Never!"

Polly was allowed to stay the night, but then she left her father's house forever. As she made her way about the countryside, begging from door to door, word of her plight reached Jack, the father of Polly's little boy. He was plagued by remorse for the irrevocable injury he had done Polly. He sent her word that there was an empty cabin on his land where she and her young son could stay. For a long while she and Billy lived there, subsisting only on corn and water.

One day Jack came to the cabin. Polly lifted Billy, by then a toddler, out of the makeshift cot and cradled him in her arms. Jack was entranced by the child, *his son*. It occurred to him that if his son ever came to despise him, it should be because of his illegitimacy and not his deprivation. Suddenly an idea was born of that thought. "I've got it. I'll take the boy to live with me. Right here and now." He leapt up and strode purposefully to the child and took him from Polly's arms. "I can do a good job as a mother," Jack said gently to Polly. "I know I can."

Although Polly was astonished, she knew Jack meant every word he said. And she knew her son would have a good home with his father. She had no milk or good food for her son, and no real home. She said a tearful good-bye to her Billy and watched as Jack carried him away.

But the boy did not thrive in the home of his father. Instead, he became so ill Jack feared for his life. Frantic, he sent for Polly. She arrived just in time to witness her son's death. Billy had learned to speak a few words, and his last words were, "My ma."

Polly's father heard from a neighbor that his grandchild had died, and the man began to worry he had been too cruel to his daughter and her child. Had the death come as a result of his turning them out of his house? Soon after Billy's death, Major Middleton died himself, without ever reconciling with his daughter. As he had made no will, Polly was awarded a child's part of his large estate.

Unexpectedly, Polly Middleton was now a woman of means. Almost everyone wished her the best in life since she surely had experienced the worst that life had to offer. But slinking around the district was a man who had an eye for any woman who was mistress of a handsome fortune. Ned Findley was known as a fortune hunter, and he set out to marry Polly.

Again, since Polly was starved for love, she found the attentions of a man rewarding. She accepted Ned Findley's proposal of marriage immediately. Almost as soon as the marriage ceremony was over, Ned began to make plans to rob Polly of her estate.

He had a cruel disposition, and it wasn't long before his mental abuse left Polly feeling inferior to everyone in the district. Findley argued continuously with Polly and whipped her with little or no provocation. Having known her father's wrath, Polly hadn't expected perfect peace in her marriage, so she accepted the abuse of her husband. Then, Ned took to drink, and in his drunken stupors he cursed and threatened her. Moreover, he moved his sister into the house and told Polly that his sister would from that moment on manage the household.

During that summer the rains set in so steady the ground couldn't hold all the water. Fields and woodlands were soon flooded. One day under a foreboding sky, Ned came in and told Polly and his sister to get ready to go to visit his friend, Mr. Gilchrist.

"In this raging storm?" Polly asked. "Are you crazy?"

"We are going to see Gilchrist and that is that," Ned answered.

"But in order to visit Mr. Gilchrist we have to go by boat," Polly cried, "and I'm still sore from the beating you gave me last night. Rowing across Stephen's Creek is more than my bruised muscles can do."

Ned looked at her with a murderous expression. "You'd better try it."

Frightened of her husband's nasty mood, Polly agreed to go, although she couldn't understand why he wanted to visit his friend at this very time. When they reached the creek, Polly tried once more to dissuade Ned. She argued that the canoe was too small to carry three people, hoping he would allow her to remain at home. But he was adamant.

Ned rowed his sister across the creek to the Gilchrist house and came back for Polly. They arrived safely, and Polly was pleasantly surprised with the welcome she received. She felt cozy and safe in the Gilchrist house and dreaded the moment she would have to leave and go back across the creek in the small boat.

The storm worsened and Mrs. Gilchrist invited the three guests to remain at her home for the night. However, Ned insisted that they leave. He wanted to get back home before complete darkness descended, he said. Again, he set out with his sister in the canoe. After a while he returned for Polly. She started to step into the small boat, but then tried to withdraw, suddenly fearful that Ned, in his black mood, would push her overboard. He screamed at her to get in, and she followed his instruction, afraid he would beat her on the spot. They pushed off.

In midstream, the tiny canoe seemed to be no match for the whirling muddy water. Polly pulled on the paddle with all her strength. Just then, Ned pulled his paddle from the water and struck Polly a vicious blow on the side of the head. She fell into the water. Ned watched her slide under the water, but in a moment she rose to the surface. Her eyes were rolling back into her head.

"For God's sake, what have I done? Don't kill me!" Polly shouted.

Blood was coming from her nose. Her cold fingers found a hold on the side of the vessel.

With the paddle, Ned smashed Polly's fingers, and she was forced to let go of the canoe. He quickly turned the boat away from her, but before he could make a getaway, Polly caught up with him. "Mercy! Have mercy!" she cried. With the last of her strength she launched herself at the canoe and got another precarious hold on the side. Maneuvering in the water, she strengthened her hold, wrapping the fingers of both hands around the rim of the canoe.

"Damn you! Damn you!" Ned screamed, furious that his plan was proving harder to execute than he had anticipated. He took his paddle and slammed it against Polly's chest and pushed her violently away. Again, she went under the water, and again she bobbed to the surface. She begged for mercy; she had no strength left to fight. Finally, Polly disappeared into the frothing water.

Mr. Gilchrist had heard poor Polly's cries and shouts, and he ran to the creek just in time to see Ned pulling Polly's body from the water on the opposite shore.

"For God's sake, Mr. Findley, what's happened?" Gilchrist shouted.

"Why nothing at all," replied Ned. "Only that my poor wife fell overboard and drowned herself."

Gilchrist quickly went to his own canoe and paddled to the opposite bank. It was now getting dark. "What are you going to do with her?" Gilchrist asked.

"Why I believe the poor soul may as well lie here where she is for the night. In the morning I'll step down with a spade and dig a bit of a grave and put her in."

Gilchrist was too shocked to reply to such a statement. But the next morning he went to the magistrate and related the whole affair as he had seen it. The magistrate rounded up some neighbors, and they arrived at the creek at the very time that Ned Findley was digging the grave. The corpse lay nearby.

A coroner's inquest was held soon afterwards, and the conclusion was Polly Findley had come to her end in a violent way. Ned was imprisoned until the day of his trial, which was brief. A physician testified the wounds and bruises on Polly's head, hands, and chest could not have come from simply falling out of a canoe and drowning. No, he said, those blows were inflicted by someone. Ned Findley was sentenced to death for the murder of his wife.

As Ned awaited the day of execution, he lost all hope for himself and was filled with pity for the deceased Polly. "I can see the looks of my poor wife while I was murdering her; and I can hear her cries! But as I had no pity on her, there is a voice which says there is none for me."

On the morning of Ned's execution, so great was his fear that he drank nearly a quart of brandy, but apparently to little effect. Those who viewed the hanging said he didn't appear to be intoxicated.

The hood was placed on Ned's head. But just at that moment, a board on which Ned was standing gave way, and he fell to the ground, some distance below him. He was pulled up, and the hood was removed. His eyes were bloodshot and weak. Tears were running down his cheeks. Ned asked for something to help him recover and was given a half a pint of liquor, which he downed in an instant.

The hood was again placed over his head, and a few minutes later Ned Findley was dead on the gallows.

There were many in Edgefield who believed Polly really died twice—"murdered" both times. They said her father killed her spirit when he rejected her, condemning her to a wretched nonlife without love or home or hope. Then, Ned Findley took her physical life from her. Murdered twice—and a miserable life in between—that was the fate of Polly Middleton.

Daddy Dearest

There was little to be cheerful about that summer of 1863 in Horry County, South Carolina. The absence of most of the able-bodied men and several years of drought coupled for a gloomy outlook. On top of that, almost everyone was scared out of their wits because of the raiders, deserters from the Confederate army who were hiding in the pine woods, lying in wait for the opportunity to attack a defenseless household and steal food and valuables.

The home in which Ellen Cooper was visiting, the home of her sister, Lou Barnhill, was a perfect target. Lou's husband was away with the militia, and the nearest neighbor lived more than a mile from their farm near Cool Spring. Besides the women, there were only two servants, whose work was to feed and care for sixty hogs. It was a frightening time. During her stay at the farm, Ellen often thought back on what Cool Spring had been like before the war.

Cool Spring was the location of one of the earliest religious campgrounds. Ellen remembered the rough shelter, which consisted of a roof supported by pilings, standing in the center of a clearing in a grove of tall pines. The shelter protected a pulpit, with benches placed all around it. Rows of adjoining roughhewn chambers called "tents" encircled the shelter. Each tent had two rooms. Nothing pleased the people of Cool Spring more than tenting on the old campground. At night the encampment was lit by lamps, and tents reflected the amber lantern glow. The scene was a spectacle after sunset, with a great number of people harmonizing as they sang the old songs. But all of that was before the war, and Ellen wondered if Cool Spring would ever again be the same. She believed not.

One dark night, the quiet was shattered by several gunshots. The next morning Mrs. Barnhill discovered two dogs had been shot; the sisters considered the killings a warning. For the next few days all was quiet in the neighborhood. Then Lou and Ellen spotted raiders in the distance. Each raider carried a gun. Upon seeing these unwelcome visitors, the sisters got to work at once to try to save their provisions. With the help of the servants, the corn, which had been stored in the barn, a building located away from the house, was moved to the smoke-house. The four then moved the large barrels of pork, several stands of lard, and fifty-nine hams.

Just after all was in place, four men arrived at the house and said they were searching for the raiders. It was common for men in the community to stop by the Barnhill farm as they searched for the outlaws. The women fervently hoped that with armed men searching for them, the raiders would leave their farm untouched. Still, the night was stretched interminably by worry.

Dawn of the following day finally came, and Ellen awoke, unaware she was about to begin a week that would be a terrible time for both her and her sister. During the day, a strange woman passed by the house several times, always walking very fast, looking neither left nor right.

"Sister, who is that woman?" Ellen always called Lou "Sister."

"I don't know her," Mrs. Barnhill replied.

"She's behaving very mysteriously, don't you think?"

"Yes. That's the third time I've seen her pass by. I've been wondering what her mission could be—"

"Oh, Sister," Ellen interrupted, "you don't suppose she could be scouting this place for the raiders!"

"Ellen, we're letting our imaginations run loose. The woman is harmless."

Still, the day passed slowly, and the sisters slept little that night as they thought of the strange woman and the likelihood of a raid at any moment. But another night passed without a raid.

Upon further consideration the next morning, Lou said she believed the best thing they could do was to take the best things in the house to the smokehouse and bury them. A massive goods box was packed with the best china, a set of cut-glass goblets, clothing, and bed linens.

While these items were being packed, a huge hole was dug in the smokehouse floor. The servants helped lower the goods box, and dirt was smoothed over it to disguise the cache. The women were pleased with their maneuver, and they decided also to bury one barrel of syrup, one of pork, and one of corn. These items were interred in barn stalls and covered with straw.

On Saturday morning, just after she had gotten out of bed, Ellen looked out and noticed what seemed to be two huge mounds of dirt piled on each side of the smokehouse door. Pulling her clothes on, she screamed for her sister. They discussed the situation but were afraid to examine the hiding places because some raiders might still be on the farm. When some minutes had passed with no noise or movement outside, they decided they would muster as much courage as possible and go to the smokehouse. Oh, how afraid they were as they made their way to the small building near the residence. Many boot tracks were in the dirt. Inside the smokehouse a hole gaped where the large box containing the china, goblets, and linens had been. The raiders had been there, but they were nowhere in sight.

"What shall we do?" Ellen cried.

"In the name of heaven, I don't know. It seems they know all we do." Mrs. Barnhill thought for a moment, then she said, "They got our good stuff, but they took no food. If they knew where the valuables were, they had to know where the food was, too."

"Do you think they will raid again?"

"I don't know, but it's clear that they have been watching us for days."

Just at that moment a voice startled the terrified women. "I hear you are in trouble. I have come to offer my help."

The women whirled about and faced a wizened man with white hair and a white beard. "Who are you?" Mrs. Barnhill questioned. "How can *you* help us?"

"I know that the raiders are coming back to take the food you have stashed away in the barn and smokehouse. If you'll let me take the food to my house, I'll save it for you."

"Who are you?" Ellen repeated her sister's question.

"Abe Rabon."

Abe Rabon! This man was offering to be their savior! Why he was a dangerous person, feared by everyone. Ellen had even viewed the hanging of his son, and she would never forget it. The execution was indelibly imprinted on her mind. She dropped her gaze, remembering. The gallows had stood in Conway where the Baptist Church was later constructed. Ellen pulled herself up to her full height and faced Rabon squarely. There was no hatred in her eyes as she spoke, but neither was there friendship. "You are kind to offer to help us," she said, a hard edge on her voice. "But I know who you are. You are a murderer."

The man nodded. "Some folks say that. But it was my son who took a life."

"My sister and I have pistols, Abe Rabon!" Mrs. Barnhill exclaimed. "If you try anything—"

"I will try nothing except to help you save your provisions. I know the raiders, and they won't be coming to my house. I can help you."

The sisters looked at each other, cautious expressions on their faces. They were suspicious of Abe Rabon, but they needed help. If the raiders came back and took the food, they would be without provisions. Could it be that this man had changed and was trying to atone for his past sins? Was it divine providence that he had appeared at this very moment? And what did they have to lose? If they didn't trust him, the raiders probably would rob them of everything anyway. On the other hand, if Abe Rabon had truly experienced regret for his misdeeds and was trying to restore his credibility, then they should trust him.

Mrs. Barnhill took the initiative. "Come to the barn," she said, leading the way. The sisters showed Rabon where they had stashed the syrup, pork, and corn in the floor of the stalls. He removed the goods and took them to his wagon. Abe climbed up into the seat. There were no parting words spoken, just a solemn exchange of looks between him and the two women before he stirred the oxen into motion.

That night Ellen and her sister stayed up all night discussing all of the stories they had heard of Abe Rabon. They would have been surprised to know that the encounter that morning had just as much effect on Abe as it had on them. Abe had not missed the flood of emotions that swept across the faces of both women. There had been fear, then courage. There had been indecision as to what course to take, then resolve. There had been accusation, then a gift of blind faith. Rabon's mind wandered as he recalled the events which were responsible for the play of emotions he had witnessed.

Before the Civil War began, Abe Rabon and his sons, Little Abe and Duke, farmed their land near Cool Spring. Another branch of the

Rabon family tree lived nearby. Big Abe thought very little of his brother and his people. He had even come up with a nickname that reflected his disdain. They were the "bad-blooded Rabons," according to Big Abe.

The area around Cool Spring was one of the state's most economically crippled sections; it was on the brink of serious decline. The whole region was suffering economic hardship. The sore between the families had been festering for some time, as each household was embittered by their own financial struggle.

"Now my brother and his young'uns are feedin' their hogs on my land," Big Abe told his sons one day. "And if you catch them at it, stop it, and I don't care how you stop it." It was not unusual for Big Abe to bully his sons. In fact, it was very common indeed.

"You mean Willie?" Little Abe asked. "I like Willie."

"You don't like nobody who feeds his hogs on our land. And you'd better get that through your head!"

"But Willie is my cousin," Little Abe countered.

"Listen to me and listen good," Big Abe shouted. "There's going to be trouble if that boy keeps on feedin' his hogs on this land. And the trouble will be for you if you see that going on and don't do nothing to stop it."

For a while there was no evidence that Abe's brother's family was feeding their swine on his property. It was the spring of 1856 and things were finally looking up for Abe. His crop looked better than it had in years. Abe kept saying he had fought long and hard to get where he was, and he wasn't going to let anyone take it away from him. He warned his children to be on the lookout for anyone or anything trespassing on his lands. They loaded all the guns in the house.

Summer was getting under way when Little Abe saw his cousin Willie feeding hogs on his father's land. Little Abe knew he had to do what his father ordered or he'd suffer the consequences. He picked up a grub stick and began to beat his cousin. He continued the assault until his cousin fell. Blood trickled from Willie's nose, ears, and mouth. He was dead. Little Abe had killed his own cousin.

Big Abe was in the living room when he heard footsteps on the front porch. Suddenly, the door was pushed inward with such force that it crashed against the wall, shaking the windowpanes. Big Abe came to his feet when he saw his son standing in the doorway, his face white and a smudge of blood on his forehead.

"Little Abe!" he cried.

His son staggered forward and fell on his knees, his breath coming in deep, laboring gasps. Between whimpers and gulps he told his story.

"He's dead! He's dead!" Little Abe cried.

"What? What are you talking about?" his father hissed.

"Willie. He was on our land feeding his pigs. I picked up a stick, and I just kept hitting him and hitting him. . . . Oh my God, what have I done?"

"You crazy maniac," Big Abe yelled at him, still bullying him. "Willie got exactly what he deserved for tryin' to fatten his hogs on the grain we've sweated to grow."

"I acted like a mad man," Little Abe uttered.

"Relax," his father admonished. "Keep calm. I'll take care of things."

A few hours later, the law arrived and charged Big Abe, Little Abe, and Duke with the killing. The three were jailed for murder.

The trial came up at the next term of criminal court. Instead of taking care of things, Big Abe made no effort to explain his role in his son's violent outburst. The whole community knew about Big Abe's threats to his own sons if they didn't protect the farm, but it looked like Little Abe was going to have to take his punishment alone. Big Abe and Duke were exonerated. Little Abe was found guilty of murder and sentenced to be hanged in June.

Immediately after the judge's sentence, Big Abe approached the bench. Everyone was stunned by his audacity when he asked the judge to change the date of the hanging. He spoke of how hard life had been on his farm. Abe explained that in recent years the crops had failed to produce food for the table, and the family was destitute. "Your honor," he pleaded, "for the first time in years, I have a good crop. I need my son, Little Abe, to help me get the crop in on time. Without his help, I won't be any better off than I have been in other years. I confess that Little Abe killed his cousin, but I give you my word. If you'll allow him to come home and work in the fields and harvest the crop in the fall, I'll see that he is at the place designated for his hanging."

The judge thought about the proposition. It was a well-known fact that in recent years there had been so little rain that many crops had failed. Farmers had a difficult time providing for their families. Rain had come in abundance during the past few months, and the water level was up again. It was likely that Big Abe was telling the truth. He needed his son to help with the farm chores. "Privilege granted," the judge said, setting the execution for a day in November.

All summer Big Abe and his two sons worked in the fields. It was a good year for corn, watermelons, and cucumbers, and there were more than enough vegetables for the table. At any mention of Little Abe's date for hanging, Big Abe would shrug. The execution was scheduled to be held at noon at the muster field in Conway. Judging from the word going around the county, it seemed that everyone was planning to attend the hanging.

November came, and while the platform was being constructed in Conway, Big Abe worked on a pine box to hold the remains of his son. A black suit was purchased for the boy's burial outfit. Suddenly, the day of execution was upon them.

Big Abe and his sons climbed onto the cart and left for the hanging. Big Abe held the reins on two oxen. The pine box was behind the men on the cart. Duke eyed his brother thoughtfully. He seemed to see Little Abe for the first time, the image softened by feelings of guilt, fear, and sentiment. Suddenly he realized just how abusive and smug their father had been. Not only had his father tormented his brother until he reacted violently, but then his father had also forced poor Abe to slave for him during his last months on earth. Big Abe noticed Duke's concern and sneered, "Little Abe asked for it." His namesake, stiff in the new black suit, said nothing, but he, too, thought about how his father had always bullied him and Duke.

Little Abe climbed up on the platform, before throngs of Low Country onlookers. A noose of rope was placed around his neck, with the knot under his chin. Someone said that the rope would drop six feet before it would become tight enough to dislocate the bones of the spinal column. A physician stood nearby.

Sheriff Johnson took over the ritual. The spectators were deathly quiet. At precisely 12:00 noon the trap was sprung. Little Abe hung limply by the neck for twenty-two minutes. Then he was lowered to the ground, and the physician pronounced him dead. Big Abe and Duke placed the body in the pine coffin, loaded it on the ox cart, and left for home. Abe buried his son, changed clothes, and went back to work.

On Sunday afternoon the sisters stayed inside, trying to keep their minds off their troubles. A knock at the door interrupted their conversation. Ellen, her spirits lifting at the prospect of a visit from one of the neighbors, skipped to the door. But it was a wounded Confederate soldier who greeted her, not a neighbor.

"Hello, miss. I wonder if I might trouble you for a drink of water."

Ellen, all of a sudden tongue-tied, could only stare. The stranger was tall, a bit ragged, and very weary. His smile made her heart leap.

"Oh, I'm sorry miss. My name is Charles Johnson." The soldier misinterpreted Ellen's silence and thought formal introductions might soften the stare of the comely young woman who faced him.

Ellen shook herself free of inertia and smiled back at him. "My name is Ellen Cooper. Won't you please come in and meet my sister?"

Johnson explained that he was returning to his home in Conway after being wounded in Virginia. The women were sympathetic and invited him to rest there for a while. When Mrs. Barnhill mentioned their trouble with the raiders, the young man offered to sit on the porch that night and guard the house. After supper, he took his position on the porch, resting his rifle across his knees. He insisted that the sisters sit well out of the way on the floor of the hall.

The frightened sisters crouched in the hall between the two front rooms of the house. All the lights had been put out, and all was quiet except for the sound of pouring rain. Each sister had a pistol in her hand. A noise startled them, but they couldn't tell from where it had come.

"What was that?" Lou whispered.

"I don't know. This is the worst night of my life."

Just then they heard shots fired and Johnson loudly cursing; he had missed his target. The women got up and ran for the porch. Another shot rang out and both Johnson and Ellen returned the fire. They didn't know whether or not they had hit their mark; they waited for another assault.

Just as suddenly as the raiders had burst into the yard, they were gone. Johnson decided to stay on guard in case they returned. The sisters sat silently, petrified and shocked. Dawn finally came as they sat side by side, rigidly still. The yard was empty. Although Johnson had fired his rifle, and he was a sharp-eyed marksman, he had killed none of the raiders in the drenching rain.

Later in the day a neighbor stopped by the house and was told about the raid. The Home Guard was notified, and a company of men came to the farm to search the surrounding woods. They discovered the woman who had passed the house, always in a big hurry. She was hiding in underbrush. After repeated questioning, she confessed that she knew where the raiders were hiding, but she would not specify the place.

The next day one of the raiders was captured and brought to the Barnhill home. He was tied to a tree and told that the punishment for a deserter from the army was death.

"What is your name?" an officer asked.

The man hedged.

"Tell us your name!"

"I won't tell you my name, but I will tell you where the provisions were taken."

"Where?"

"The raiders all live around here. They took the food to their homes."

"Give us the names of the raiders."

"No."

"*What is your name?*"

The man hung his head. He knew they'd find out soon enough. "Duke Rabon."

"Big Abe Rabon's son? The man who should have been the one on the end of a rope, but he let his son hang?"

"The one and the same."

"And is your dad the ringleader of this gang of raiders?"

"The one and the same," Duke repeated.

"Your dad always was . . ."

"A bully," Duke finished for him.

When the sisters realized Abe Rabon not only wasn't honest, he was the ringleader of the raiders, they figured their provisions were gone for good. And they felt both foolish and embarrassed that they had placed their faith in such a man.

Curiously, though, Rabon hadn't told any of his fellow outlaws about his visit to the Barnhill place. That's why they raided it again, even though the food was no longer there. And before Abe was captured and taken to Conway to be jailed with the other raiders, he returned the provisions to the sisters. Again, there were no words between them, only a solemn exchange of looks, and the sisters knew their gift of faith wasn't wasted after all.

The worst night of Ellen's life had another sunny side as well. A strong bond formed between Johnson and Ellen that long and harrowing night when both had fired guns at the raiders. A few months later, on a peaceful and golden day, they were married.

The Man Who Escaped His Own Grave

In 1867 Dr. C. M. Van Poole witnessed the hanging of Rufus Ludwig in Rowan County, North Carolina. What he saw that day affected him so much that years later Dr. Poole felt compelled to write an account of that hanging and burial. It was Dr. Poole's belief that Rufus Ludwig escaped from his own grave.

Dr. Van Poole wasn't the only one of that opinion. Many spectators were present at both the hanging and the burial. There were even rumors several weeks after the hanging that Rufus's court-appointed attorneys had just received a letter from him. It supposedly read: "I am under many obligations for your efforts in my behalf, but I find there is more dependence to be put in slack ropes and shallow graves than in lawyers." Rufus certainly had a sense of humor.

In spite of all this, a combination of horror and embarrassment kept most of the speculation to private whispers for almost seventy years. Widespread public discussions began only after Dr. Van Poole published his account of the hanging shortly before his death in 1933.

It all began, witnesses said, when the wagon backed up to the scaffold and the rear gate was removed. The sheriff walked up to Rufus and asked him if he had anything to say.

"My mother asked me if the gun was well loaded and I told her that it was," Rufus answered. It was a curious and surprising remark for someone to make only minutes before his death. "And I want to sing some hymns with you," Rufus added.

"Any special hymn?" the sheriff questioned.

Rufus answered and the strains of "Lord, Dismiss Us with Thy Bless-ing" filled the town. Some hummed along, and one woman sang powerfully in a minor key. She held her hands above her head, and her body began to sway as Ludwig intoned, "Lord, dismiss us with thy bless-ing; fill our hearts with joy and peace. Let us each, thy love possessing, triumph in redeeming grace. . . ."

"Come on, Rufus," the sheriff yelled. "It's time for your hanging. I'll walk up the steps beside you."

Rufus jumped out of the wagon, and the sheriff held his arm as they started up the steps to the scaffold. Just at that moment, Rufus made a tremendous lunge for freedom, jumping from the elevated platform to the ground. He stumbled. Managing to pull himself up before any-one grabbed him, he began to run. He was running for his life when large hands clamped down on his shoulders. Rufus wiggled away from the hands. Another hand caught his elbow and pulled him to the ground.

"He's going to escape his own hanging," someone called out to no one in particular.

"All his life he's been unusual," Joshua Clement answered. "He has a reputation for doing the unexpected, and I'll wager there'll be some sort of revelation at the end."

"Well, I don't know," another bystander took up the conversation. "The sheriff's got him now and there's no getting away."

"Want to speculate on that?" Clement asked.

"No bet," the man answered, shaking his head. "I have to stretch my pennies too much to take a chance on Rufus Ludwig."

Several other men climbed up on the platform to help the sheriff. Rufus was held while the noose was placed around his neck. "He al-ways was a no-good," one of the helpers remarked.

He wasn't alone in this sentiment. It had always been said of Ludwig that he had few admirable traits. In this respect, he was like his ances-tors. Rufus Ludwig was the only son of Mathias and Dicie Ludwig, and the word most often used to describe his mother was "evil." But Rufus came from a long line of scoundrels that included an uncle who was hanged for murdering his wife, a cousin who had gained notoriety as a thief, another cousin who died at the gallows for murdering his mother-in-law, and an ancestor who had crossed enemy lines during the Civil War and joined ranks with the Union troops.

When Rufus himself reached military age, he was taken against his wishes and forced to join the Confederate army. Although he had reluctantly joined the militia, he actually seemed to look forward to his first encounter with the enemy. The other men in his company wondered about this. He hadn't a grain of patriotism in his body, and yet he wanted to confront the Yankees. Word came that the Yankees would try to take a nearby stronghold, and Rufus's company was ordered to defend it. Unknown to Rufus, his associates had become interested in how he would behave in battle. They kept their eyes on him.

Just as the Federals approached and began firing, Rufus raised his muzzleloading rifle. A moment before he pulled the trigger, he placed the fingers of his right hand over the muzzle. A grimace spread over his face as he pulled the trigger, blowing away the fingers of his right hand at the middle joints.

For days he lay in an ill-equipped and badly staffed hospital, his hand wrapped in a blood-soaked rag. His body was racked with pain. Medical science had not yet discovered the importance of antiseptics in preventing infection, and many thousands of men were dying from wounds and disease. But Rufus was a survivor. As soon as he was strong enough, he fled from the hospital and hid out at his father's home near the junction of Dutch Second Creek and the Yadkin River. While there, he was depressed, moody, and still suffering from his self-inflicted wound.

One day there was a knock at the door. Rufus opened it and found himself staring into the stern face of a Confederate soldier.

"We're looking for Rufus Ludwig," the soldier said, not recognizing Rufus, who was ill, and thin from malnutrition.

"Who?"

"Rufus Ludwig. He has no discharge. He deserted."

Rufus glanced at his heavily bandaged hand. Some other Confederate soldiers had joined the one questioning him. They, too, were looking at his injured hand.

"Rufus Ludwig contrived an injury," a militiaman remarked. "He has only half fingers on his right hand. Would you expose your right hand?"

Rufus felt like a trapped animal with no place to flee. "I am Rufus Ludwig," he admitted, realizing there was no immediate route of escape. He left with the soldiers, but before reaching Salisbury, he slipped away from them and remained in hiding for several days. They returned to their company. When they reported that Ludwig had made a getaway, it was decided there could be no further effort to capture him. The conflict between the North and South was at its peak. The men who had pursued Ludwig were needed for battle.

Strangely enough, this ne'er-do-well later began to court Miss Commilla Campbell, a young woman of much beauty. She came from a distinguished family whose every member discouraged her interest in Rufus. No one could understand Commilla's attraction to Rufus. After all, it was widely known that he had shot off parts of his fingers in order to evade fighting for the cause. But there was something about him that intrigued Commilla.

"You will regret it for the rest of your life if you marry that scoundrel," her father protested.

"Our family will live under the scandal for a hundred years and more," her mother added.

"Miss Milla," her body servant cautioned, "you marry that man, you don't have no sense a-tall. Can't trust him. He got more trick than the law 'low."

But Rufus was very persuasive, and Commilla married him. After their wedding, the couple went to live with Rufus's parents. His mother, called "Old Dicie" by the neighbors, had a tantrum over the marriage and refused to let Commilla come inside the house. Commilla was forced to flee into the woods, and she remained there for weeks. Several people went to see her in the woods and to talk with her in an effort to soothe her over her failed marriage.

Commilla had been married seven weeks, hiding in the woods and relying on friends to bring her food and clean clothing, when one day a friend convinced Commilla to go home with her. "Old Dicie is evil," the woman cautioned. "Don't go back there."

"Why did I every marry Rufus?" Commilla cried. "My family, even my maid, warned me about the Ludwigs. But I couldn't see what they were talking about then. Now it is very clear. I wish my father knew how I have come to feel."

After much deliberation Commilla decided to go home and face her father. "You have been disowned!" he shouted. "We begged you not to marry that outlaw, but you wouldn't listen to us. You made your bed, now you can lie on it."

Commilla left her parents' home, more dejected than she had believed was possible. There was nowhere to go but back to Rufus. He told her that he loved her and promised her that his family would take her in as soon as he spoke with his mother. He arranged to meet Commilla in the woods and promised that they would go fishing and, later, pick wild strawberries. Commilla was once again hopeful that things might work out for them.

But happiness was not Commilla's fate. While she and Rufus strolled through the woods, Commilla bent over to pick some sweet strawberries. It was then that Rufus shot her in the back of the head. She toppled forward, sprawled out in the strawberry patch. Rufus ran home and got his mother and sister, Jane. They flew back to the scene, with Old Dicie carrying a butcher knife.

Commilla had pulled herself to a nearby tree and was sitting by it, the tree supporting her back. Her face was smeared with blood.

"Jane," Rufus's mother said, "if you'll slit that girl's throat with this butcher knife, I'll give you a bushel of wheat."

Jane, being an obedient daughter, gave Commilla's throat a whack. It had never occurred to Jane to disregard her mother's orders. Both of Old Dicie's children did everything they could to please her. As long as they could remember, neither of them had ever crossed her. When Rufus realized that he had married a girl whom his mother would not welcome into the household, he had to do away with the young wife. It was the only way Old Dicie would have it.

After performing her gory task, Jane flew home and got a sheet. When she returned to the scene of the murder, she, Dicie, and Rufus wrapped the remains of the young bride in the sheet.

Commilla had been missing for nine days when an old woman, Julia Hartman, noticed a concentration of buzzards while she was out for a walk. Julia hurried home and formed a search party of local men.

On June 17, 1867, an article in the Carolina Watchman reported that Commilla's body had been found with a slit throat and a rifle wound to the head.

Rufus was immediately arrested. Later, there was some mystery as to why Old Dicie and Jane weren't indicted with him. Speculation ran along several lines. One explanation was that the murder took place right after the Civil War, when lawlessness was more common than lawfulness. Also, arresting members of the "fairer sex" wasn't exactly popular at that time. A more convincing argument may be that the extent of the Ludwig women's involvement wasn't widely known until much later. Besides, Rufus probably wouldn't have implicated his own family since it would have done nothing to mitigate his own guilt.

There was only circumstantial evidence against him until Rufus himself was trapped into confessing the crime. While questioning him in his jail cell, the constable asked Rufus why he had put the body in the river. When Rufus corrected the man by saying he did not put the body in the river, but in the creek, his fate was sealed. At least everyone thought so.

Now Rufus stood on the platform, ready to pay the consequences. The trap was sprung. The scaffold dropped. Rufus swung to and fro, his breath coming in irregular gasps.

"His neck didn't break," an onlooker yelled.

Rufus hung by the neck for nineteen minutes, then it was suggested that he be taken down and placed in the coffin. Dr. Van Poole offered to accompany the remains to the Ludwig farm for burial.

Just before the coffin was lowered into the newly dug grave at the Ludwig farm, Dr. Van Poole suggested that the top of the coffin be opened for a last look. When the coffin was opened, Rufus Ludwig did not have the look of death. And he was warm to the touch. The men looked at one another. What did you do in a case like this? Have another hanging? That would be inconceivable, they thought. Maybe they were mistaken. Surely he was dead after all. The top of the coffin was slammed shut.

The casket was lowered into the grave and dirt was shoveled over it. Before the gaping hole had been filled, there came from the coffin such a racket that the men threw down their shovels and stared at each other. Rufus's relatives had puzzled expressions on their faces, but they did not insist that the coffin be opened.

The men who had built the scaffold and carried out the hanging found themselves in their own particular kind of hell. The government had encouraged them to carry out an execution, and now, through no fault of their own, they were left to work out the macabre details. They wondered what they should do. The whole county would register horror when it was learned that a man had been intentionally buried alive. Suddenly, as if of one will, the men hurriedly filled the grave with dirt and left the site. If Rufus still lived, then his family could pull him from the coffin and decide what to do with him. After all, the authorities had done their best to hang the man, and if he didn't die it wasn't their fault. Right at that moment they wanted nothing more than to be rid of the problem.

Several days later, a man snooped back to the gravesite on the Ludwig farm. Dirt lay in a mound by the vacant hole, with the conspicuously empty coffin nearby. Word soon spread about the countryside that Rufus Ludwig had come back from the grave. Not only that, but his whole family had disappeared too. The Ludwigs never returned, and it wasn't until Dr. Van Poole told his story in 1933 that all of the facts and rumors about what had really happened at that grave in 1867 were openly told.

Death at Little Black Creek Swamp

There is a cold spell that descends on North Carolina each February, when icy winds roar across the mountains, freeze the Piedmont, and break and scatter the brittle limbs of the live oaks along the coast. That's the time of year to flame a fire on the hearth and settle in until the freeze blows on over the Atlantic.

It was on such a night in 1875 that Alfred Winfield Partin, Jr., who was called Scott by everyone who knew him, chose to take his wife and infant daughter from their home at Panther Branch to visit his cousin, who lived close to Garner Station, a small community near Raleigh. Although it was a three-mile walk in the bitter wind at night, Scott seemed determined to go. "I know this district like the back of my hand," he said.

"Did you have to choose this night for the visit?" his wife asked as they walked out the door.

"I feel like seeing my people again," Scott answered. He picked up a tow sack before leaving the yard and threw it over a shoulder.

"See people!" his wife snapped, holding the baby to her chest to keep the small bundle warm.

"There's a promise of thaw tomorrow."

"Thaw!" she spat. "Frost'll be over my ankles when we come back this way."

Bent forward against the wind, he cajoled, "Keep your mind on the fresh-baked bread and hot tea we'll get when we arrive."

Arguing is futile, she thought. There's no alternative. Perhaps she *would* think of the bread and tea likely to be served to them. It was better than dwelling on her half-frozen hands and feet.

Soon he was walking so fast along the road, which was full of hills and curves, that he was able to glance at her only now and then. Gradually he picked up speed, and she couldn't even hear what he said anymore. His gaze seemed fixed on the crest of a hill and the bare treetops beyond.

"Wait for us," she called out, but Scott didn't seem to hear. "Wait!"

He leaned forward against the wind and pressed on.

"Wait for us. Help me with the baby. I can't carry her any longer. My hands are stiff."

Finally he turned and started back. As she handed him the child, the baby was dropped. Her head struck the frozen ground.

The woman dropped to the ground and grabbed the child and held her up, gently pressing the baby to her face. Something slimy wet stuck to her cheek. Blood! She felt the child's face, her hands going to the nose, mouth, eyes, forehead. All strength drained from her body as she realized the truth. "You've killed her! You've *killed* her." She felt as though she was going to collapse.

"Shut your fool mouth!"

"Oh, God almighty," she cried, close to hysteria. "You've killed my . . ."

"I said to shut up." Scott's teeth were clenched as he snarled at his wife, but she was beyond noticing. She remained on her knees, gently rocking her tiny daughter and keening into the wind.

Scott eyed the road, up and down. No one was in sight. He took the child from his wife and pushed the baby into the tow sack.

"No!" his wife screamed. "Don't put her in a sack! What are you *doing*? Are you crazy?"

Maybe Scott *was* crazy—or angry, or scared. Or his next actions may have been premeditated. Whatever the case, he dropped the sack to the ground and grabbed his wife by the neck and started choking her. She tried to push him away, but she had no feeling in her palms and fingers. They wouldn't function. Her arms felt like cold pipes. Just as she lost consciousness, she was trying to hit his face with the pipes.

The night seemed angry. The wind was building, cold. Trees were tossing in abandon, and limbs were snapping. Scott grabbed his wife's limp arms and pulled her over the hard ground off the road and through the trees. He was young—only twenty-seven years old—but he weighed just 135 pounds, and his strength was nearly spent when, finally, he reached a clearing, Little Black Creek Swamp. Scott stretched his wife on the ground and went back for the sack. He placed the baby on his wife's chest. Both were as cold and still as marble. He walked about, gathering dead wood. The limbs and twigs were cold, but dry. Scott stacked them over the woman and child.

He tried to light a fire, but it wouldn't catch. He started it again, but again it fizzled. Drat such wind! Scott looked at the tow sack, but decided not to use it. Looking about, he found some other twigs. After breaking them into small pieces, he was able to start a fire. A flare danced up, and a flicker darted in another direction. Scott stood back, staring at the funeral pyre. But just at that moment, a gust scattered the brush and blew the fire out.

Furious, Scott stamped his feet and cursed into the wind. Then, he reached for his hunting knife. Quickly and methodically, he cut up his wife and child until he believed they would fit in the tow sack. But his wife's legs protruded. He broke them. His hands were now so cold they wouldn't work well, but he managed to push everything into the sack.

He picked up the heavy load and stumbled over to the creek. It looked to be frozen. What the heck? He pitched the sack into the water and heard ice break, followed by a sucking, gurgling sound. Scott ran home, his breath coming out as white vapor. When he arrived, his mother was sleeping.

"Mother. Wake up."

She mumbled, still half asleep.

He touched her shoulder. "Mother, wake up."

"Hmmm? Is that you son?"

"Yes. I want to tell you that I'm going to move my wife and daughter to the next county."

"In this weather? Now? It's cold. Go back to sleep."

"I haven't been to sleep. I'm going to take the trunk for our clothes."

"You can have the trunk, but you're making a mistake." She pulled a quilt over her shivering head.

Nothing happened for a few weeks. Then J. H. H. Walton, Scott's father-in-law, became concerned. His daughter had always kept in touch with him. It wasn't like her to miss her regular visits. He went to the house where she had lived. Scott's mother told him that her son and his wife had moved to another county. Walton thought about his son-in-law, a no-good man, and he became suspicious. "When did they move?"

"On the night of the freeze."

"Which night? The freeze lasted three days."

"The first night."

"Have you heard from them?"

"No."

"Something about this doesn't set well with me," Walton said. "My daughter wouldn't have left without saying good-bye."

"So?"

"So I'm going to tell the authorities and then I'm going to hunt for her myself, starting right now."

Walton went about the countryside with one thing on his mind— finding his daughter and grandchild. When he described them to strangers along the way, he said, "My daughter is a good girl, a church-going girl. She's fragile and delicate. I couldn't ask for a better girl. Her child is a baby girl." When he was questioned about Scott, he answered, "A scoundrel with a downcast look and a bad temper. Don't know what she wanted with him. He used to be a prison guard. Besides that, he has four scars on his body."

Both Walton and the authorities searched for the family in vain. Then, five months later, Little Black Creek Swamp revealed its secret. Partin's wife and child, or what remained of them, were discovered when some men, who were trying to rake a drowned cow from the black and swampy water, pulled out the gory tow sack.

The authorities interviewed Scott's neighbors and friends. Several reported that the upper part of the index finger on Partin's right hand was missing. Someone else said he walked parrot-toed. These facts were added to the description Walton had given them.

Four hundred dollars was offered as reward for Scott Partin. It was a goodly sum for 1875, and many people daydreamed about collecting the money. For months, everybody was on the lookout for the suspect.

Thirteen years passed. Most people had forgotten about Scott Partin and the reward money. But, unbeknownst to the general public, Solicitor Argo of Wake County and Governor Scales had hired detectives to shadow a man who fit the description of the murderer.

On Saturday, June 23, 1888, a tramp who looked something like Partin was arrested in Selma, North Carolina. He said his name was John William Henry Scott. During the interrogation that followed, the prisoner said he had been working up North in the mines until recently. After he'd moved down South, he ran into trouble with his landlady. She kept fussing about his temper. She stood it as long as she could, then she told him she was evicting him and set a day for him to move out of her house. As the tramp recalled the incident, he spoke angrily, saying he had threatened that he "would like to cut her to pieces and burn her up!" This remark startled the law enforcement officers who heard it. The man was Scott Partin for sure! They examined the suspect and discovered four scars on his body exactly like those Walton had described, and the upper part of the index finger on his right hand was missing. A telegram was dispatched to Solicitor Argo in Raleigh. "We have Scott Partin. Has been identified by many."

Mr. Upchurch, clerk of superior court for Wake County, reopened the case. The prisoner was scheduled to be returned to Raleigh for questioning; he would arrive on the midnight train on June 26.

Emotions were running high about the man who had so brutally murdered his wife and chopped up not only her body but that of his own child. There was talk of a lynching among the curious bystanders waiting at the railroad station.

Stifling hot weather usually doesn't settle on North Carolina until late July or August. But that year it descended on the region in June. Not a breeze was stirring at the railroad station. The heat didn't do anything to improve the brooding mood of the people waiting to get their hands on Scott Partin.

Near midnight, while the onlookers were waiting expectantly, the train clanged to a stop miles away on the outskirts of town. The lynch talk had reached the officers in charge of the prisoner, so they made arrangements for the train to be stopped where the tracks crossed Fayetteville Street. A patrol carriage to transport the fugitive was waiting there.

A man walking by the patrol carriage studied the prisoner's stride as he walked from the train to the carriage. "By his parrot-toed walk, I'd know that one anywhere," he declared. "It's Scott Partin."

By the time the train arrived at the station, the people waiting had worked themselves up to a feverish pitch. The first passenger who emerged from the train had to withdraw as the mob surged toward him. Finally, all the passengers had left the train, but Scott Partin wasn't among them. The onlookers were furious. Someone yelled, "To the jailhouse," and they flew in that direction. "We've been tricked," another man called out as he ran. When they arrived at the jail, Sheriff Rogers told the angry crowd the prisoner was locked up and nobody could see him until the next day.

The next morning the Raleigh *News and Observer* carried a story about the prisoner's arrival and the mob's surge from the depot to the jail. "It was a strange sight to see a long line of humanity pouring through the city at the midnight hour."

When the prisoner was questioned, he spoke with an Irish brogue and declared that his name was Leeson Porter, not John Scott as he had said in Selma. He claimed that he had arrived in this country in 1873 on the steamer *Hibernia*.

Someone knew an Irishman who lived in the vicinity, so he was sent for immediately.

"What are they feeding you?" he asked.

"I don't get porridge here," the captive answered.

Porridge, the Irishman thought. Local people called it oatmeal. "Do you eat potatoes?" the Irishman continued his questioning.

"I eat potatoes. Did you know about the famine in the forties?"

"Yes," the Irishman answered reflectively. If the prisoner knew about the potato famine, then he surely was an Irishman. They talked more.

"The worst disaster in Irish history," the prisoner went on. "When the blight hit the potatoes and destroyed them, more than seven hundred thousand people died."

The questioner thought about all the man had said. Now and then the prisoner had used Gaelic words, like *abainn* for river, and *baile* for town. There was no doubt in the Irishman's mind as to the homeland of the prisoner.

A Raleigh citizen who had known Partin well was also asked to interview the jailed man. After they chatted for more than two hours, the man from Raleigh announced that he was certain the prisoner was Partin, the accused murderer.

Was he Partin or wasn't he? That was the question of the day. Dozens of people came to pass their opinions on his identity. Some were not sure, while others were absolutely positive in their identification. The missing half-finger was pointed out, and the prisoner had scars identical to those of Partin. As the day progressed and the ragged man was subjected to the probing eyes and questions of one person after another, he grew increasingly agitated. He shouted to his accusers that he was innocent.

The following day, Wednesday, June 27, two men arrived who had been ordered to examine the prisoner: Walton, Partin's father-in-law, and Mr. Utley, a close acquaintance. Many believed the true identity of the prisoner certainly would be decided then. Before their arrival, the prisoner was ordered to clean himself up because he was so filthy the dirt obscured his features. He shaved, washed himself, and dressed in a new suit of clothes provided for the occasion.

Upon seeing the prisoner, Walton shook his head. "This man's not Partin," he said. "Partin had blue eyes. Look at those eyes. They're brown. Scott had a squint in his eyes. This man's eyes are open. And this man's hair is reddish. Scott's was brown. And I never knew Partin had a part of his finger missing."

Utley echoed the conclusion. There was a collective moan. The other people in the room had at first looked on with amusement, but now they seemed outraged, cheated. They filed out of the jail and told the people standing in groups outside that the man was not Partin.

As the days passed, photographs of the two men were compared. The men looked remarkably similar. The prisoner was ordered to write something, and it was compared to letters Partin had written. The handwriting, too, was very similar. Still, there was no concrete evidence. The prisoner became even more agitated and moody.

It was on a day when the man was relatively calm that Solicitor Argo questioned him.

"Who are you?"

The man settled back in a chair. "I am Robert Leeson Porter. I was born in Queen's County, Ireland, on July 22, 1850. On July 2, 1873, I sailed from Queenstown on the steamer *Hibernia*. After landing in Nova Scotia I went to work in a piano warehouse owned by Charles Hood. After leaving Nova Scotia, I joined the United States Army at Fort Perble, Maine. I was stationed there for two years, and on December 30, 1877, I was discharged at Fort Barrancas, Florida."

Argo flew back to his office to check out the information. He immediately wrote to William Endicott, the secretary of war, in Washington, D. C., and to the American consul in Ireland. But the information Argo desired didn't come quickly. In the days that followed, reporters from the newspaper pestered the solicitor, but there was still no news from the secretary of war or the American consul.

More and more statements of identification were made. John Lewis Johnson, who had known Scott quite well, said he was absolutely certain the prisoner was the murderer. J. A. Surles pointed out that he had worked with Partin three days before the murders, and the man held in jail was the man with whom he had raked straw. In late July another large group of people who had known Partin arrived at the jail to take a look at the man in question. They all eyed him carefully. Some said he was Scott Partin; others were not certain.

Later in the month, word finally came from the army, from Lieutenant McCallum, adjutant of the Fifth Artillery Division. He said he had seen a photograph of the prisoner, and he would swear that it was Robert Leeson Porter, formerly of the United States Army.

On Tuesday morning, July 31, at nine o'clock in the morning, Porter walked out of the jailhouse, a free man. He hung around the area for three days, talking to those who had become interested in the case. Then, under the cover of darkness one night, he fled.

Two weeks after he left Raleigh, the *News and Observer* ran an item that had been carried in the *New York World* on August 12, 1888. It seemed that Robert Leeson Porter was a member of an aristocratic Irish family with members in the British peerage. An international search had been going on to find him because he had inherited land and a large sum of money.

When Porter was found near Portsmouth, Virginia, he was half dead from malnutrition and fatigue. As he regained his health, Porter began to show interest in his legacy. He soon left for New York and there boarded a vessel for Ireland.

To this day, no one knows what happened to Scott Partin. But everyone knows he got away with murder.

A Love Triangle, Victorian-Style

A bleak shroud of darkness covered the sea as Francis Warrington Dawson leaned against the rail of the ship. He had no misgivings about this move from England to America. His sympathies had been with the Confederacy since the moment he had heard about Fort Sumter. As he stood on deck with waves spraying his face, Dawson began to plan how he would establish himself in Charleston. He liked what he had heard of the place; Charleston was reported to be much like London, and many Charlestonians collected furniture that was known for its craftsmanship. If things went as planned, after the war he could add to his own collections. Dawson left the deck and went to his cabin to check on the heirlooms he was bringing to America. Tapping a crate with a finger, he felt certain the people he would get to know would appreciate his taste in furniture and art.

But first there was a war to fight. Dawson's vessel had not been docked for very long before Dawson found that fighting, even for the Confederate cause, was far more hideous than he had envisioned. However gruesome and ghastly the war was to him, Dawson managed to do everything that was expected of a hero. He was commissioned an officer; he fought at Gettysburg; he was wounded in action. His entry into Charleston society was assured.

After the war, Captain Francis Warrington Dawson settled into a house on Bull Street and was accepted as a son of Charleston. It was known far and wide that Charleston society was organized by pedigrees, and Dawson's social advancements came more easily and quickly than he had anticipated. Although the destinies of many in Charleston society had been controlled by Middletons, Draytons, Alstons, and Edmondstons before the war, these families were no longer so exclusive as to shut out the dashing young war hero.

Dawson's new home reflected his excellent taste in fine furnishings and *objets d'art*. On the sideboard he displayed a richly ornamented silver teapot which had been made by a woman silversmith, a member of the London Guild. On his shelves were numerous books on sports that he had acquired in London bookstalls, including *British Rural Sports; Stonehenge Sportsman's Cyclopedia*, Volumes 1 and 2; and *The History of the Turf*.

But Captain Dawson was not satisfied solely with being a Charleston gentleman. He began looking for the sort of business endeavor that would be appropriate for him. Over glasses of ale, Dawson discussed several propositions, until he finally settled on buying an interest in the *Charleston News*. In 1872, the paper merged with the *Daily News*, and the *Charleston News and Courier* was born.

By this time, Dawson had also become a husband and father. As his family increased, he secured the services of a governess for the little ones. The dainty and petite Swiss governess, Marie Burdayton, seemed perfect for the job. She was very well qualified for the post, but Dawson could hardly have failed to be swayed, at least a little, by her astonishing good looks. She cut quite a fashionable figure when strolling the streets of Charleston. When she ventured out, she was usually attired in a snug-fitting dress of black, trimmed in white. The frilly white ruffles on the sleeves nearly concealed her tiny hands. Her favorite hat had a wide brim, and the white feathers that embellished it contrasted with the black crown.

Soon it developed that as Marie passed by on her daily stroll, many a heavy damask drapery was pulled back as admiring or envious eyes took in her coquettish walk. There was no question but that she was the most beautiful woman in Charleston, and many Charlestonians had already begun to gossip. It was whispered in nearly every drawing room that nice Captain Dawson had an eye for his children's governess. At first most people had believed his attentions simply to be a fatherly interest, but then one night someone had seen a profile of Captain Dawson kissing Marie as they stood before a ceiling-to-floor window. As they left the window, Captain Dawson's arm was around Marie's shoulders, and soon afterward all lamps in the house were extinguished.

Gossip about Captain Dawson and Marie had peaked and was diminishing when the possibility of a new romantic intrigue suddenly surfaced. For a few weeks, Charlestonians had noticed that Marie's strolls were taking her in a different direction, always in the neighborhood of Dr. McDow. A buzz of scandal rocked Charleston when it was rumored that Marie had been observed kissing Dr. McDow as she left his office one day. Marie was more than naughty; both of the men were married. Surely Dr. McDow had heard the rumor about Marie and her employer? And what would Captain Dawson think when he found out? So the gossip went, spicing up life in the port city.

Although the people of Charleston had given Captain Dawson the benefit of the doubt, they were convinced of Dr. McDow's guilt. But until then, the reputation of Dr. Thomas Ballard McDow had been unimpeachable. He had done his undergraduate work at the University of Lebanon, in Tennessee, where he graduated with first honors. His graduate work had been done at the Medical College of South Carolina, in Charleston, where he also graduated with honors and was valedictorian of his class. His father, Dr. R. S. McDow, practiced medicine in Lancaster, South Carolina. But if it was true that the good doctor had given Marie a gold watch and a copy of that obscene book, *Twixt Love and Law*, then the city had a downright scandal on its hands. After all, Dr. McDow was married.

His marriage to a German woman had brought him a handsome dowry. It was with that dowry that Dr. and Mrs. McDow built the luxurious home that brought them into the sacred circle of the socially elite. Charlestonians usually snubbed their noses at self-made men, only allured by those who could set the current fashion by giving a few good parties in a house that gave full view of their treasures. The McDow home was the epitome of that tradition.

The house itself was a typical antebellum Charleston single house of solid brick, with eaves undergirded by ornamental brickwork. Over-window "eyebrows" in three styles graced the structure. The three porches, one atop another, were cooled on three sides by bay breezes. With its symmetry and variety of ornamentation—its gables, dormers, balusters, and delicate Victorian filigree—the house was an outstanding addition to Charleston architecture. Dr. McDow so enjoyed his house that he practiced medicine in the basement.

In the center of his waiting room was a round table piled high with medical books and journals. If one had cared to check, the books included *System of Surgery; Etiquette for Gentlemen; System of Medicine*

Practice; On the Chest; Medical Dictionary; Elements of Physiology; Chemistry for Students; and *Therapeutics.* Behind his big desk was a regular apothecary stocked with bottles filled with black and gold liquids, and a brass mortar and pestle. Bottles of mace, boracic, coccus, and ipecac were placed alongside empty bottles waiting to be filled.

It was into this office that Captain Dawson marched one fine spring afternoon in March. Someone had told him that Marie was "involved in some sort of misconduct with Dr. McDow" and was perhaps at the doctor's office that very moment. Captain Dawson wasted no time in racing over to the McDow home. He couldn't have guessed that before the sun went down, one man would be dead and another man ruined.

The people of Charleston heard the shocking news the next morning, March 13, 1889. The *News and Courier* carried a bombshell headline: "Captain Dawson Murdered." Several subheads read:

The news that shocked all Charleston last night.

Killed early in the afternoon by Dr. T. B. McDow
in the office of the latter.

Murderer remained locked up two hours
with body of victim.

An attempt at secret burial.

Failure and subsequent surrender to the police.

The article went on to report that at about half past three o'clock the day before, Captain Dawson had left his office. It had been brought to his attention that one of his domestics, a stranger in America, was involved somehow in improper conduct with Dr. McDow. Since Marie's conduct and welfare were his responsibility, Captain Dawson went to Dr. McDow's office. The article went on to say that Captain Dawson had the best reasons for calling upon Dr. McDow, where he might find it necessary to defend Marie's honor.

From his jail cell, Dr. McDow explained that Captain Dawson entered his office in a rage and knocked him down with his walking cane. McDow got up, grabbed his gun, and shot Dawson. He lived for nearly an hour, during which time the doctor remained in the room, trying to decide what to do. After Dawson expired, Dr. McDow stayed in the room for another hour, still trying to make up his mind about what to do with the body. Finally, it came to him. He would bury the corpse.

At the end of a passageway outside the office there was a half-door opening into a recess under a stairway. The floor terminated at a place that left a rather large space of ground. Dr. McDow pulled the victim to the end of the floor and began to dig a grave. When the hole was deep enough to hold the body, Dr. McDow rolled the corpse into it. For some period of time, the doctor couldn't say how long, he just stood there, still pondering. He came to the conclusion that he would be better off if he would plead self-defense. He pulled the body out of the hole and back into his office, where he made a feeble attempt to clean it. In his account, Dr. McDow went on to say that at about seven o'clock in the evening, he became fully aware of the crime he had committed and turned himself in to the authorities.

Dr. Middleton Michel was sent to the physician's office to perform an autopsy. Dawson's face had one or two abrasions, and a large bloodstain was found on his shirt. On closer examination of the body, Dr. Michel found the fatal wound. The bullet entered the body, going parallel with the ridge of the hipbone. There was evidence of an internal hemorrhage, and it was discovered that the vena cava, the large vein that discharges blood into the right atrium of the heart, had been severed.

All of Charleston was abuzz with news of the murder. Although a terrible storm was flooding the streets of Charleston on the day of the inquest, the courtroom was filled to capacity. A trembling Dr. McDow, a mere shell of the professional man he had been only a few days earlier, was led to a chair. The McDow case was scheduled for trial in the June term of the court of general session for Charleston County. Judge Kershaw of the Fifth Judicial Circuit was assigned to hear the case.

On Monday morning, June 24, 1889, throngs of spectators filled the hallways and jammed the stairways and sidewalk. It was the largest crowd ever to assemble to hear a case being tried in Charleston. Dr. McDow was placed in the prisoner's dock. Reporters who were covering the story included those from the *New York Sun*, the *Augusta Chronicle*, and the *New York World*.

The case began at ten o'clock. Seven blacks and five whites were chosen for the jury. The first witness was the physician who performed the autopsy. His testimony concerned the path of the bullet. Dr. Michel explained that the bullet's line of flight was from behind; the prosecutor began an effort to prove that Dawson had been shot in the back. The next witness was the deputy coroner, C. H. Rivers, who gave a description of the scene as he found it. This testimony was followed by that of Coroner John DeVeaux, who revealed that he had found a bloodstained towel and a Smith and Wesson pistol with one chamber fired. He had taken the pistol from McDow's desk. He then described the freshly dug hole in the sand at the end of the passageway. There had been footprints and blood in the hole. The court adjourned for the day.

In the hallways and out on the street, the talk was of the jury. No one seemed to believe that Dr. McDow would receive justice. "You know Dr. McDow doesn't stand a chance," someone said. "With the war still fresh in their minds, black jurors won't free a white man." "They won't listen to his plea of self-defense," another added.

About noon the next day, an unexpected witness was called to the stand. Marie Burdayton made her way slowly and deliberately to the front of the courtroom. She approached the bench in her clinging black dress and wide-brimmed hat. She smiled at the judge. Since Marie's first language was French, there was some difficulty in explaining what was meant by kissing the Bible before giving evidence. However, she soon began her testimony, relating what she called the truth. As she spoke, Marie touched her cheek with her tiny hand, wreathed in white lace.

"How old are you?"

"Twenty-two."

"Has Dr. McDow ever kissed you?"

"Yes."

"How many times?"

"Two times."

A lawyer held up the novel, *Twixt Love and Law*. It was a Victorian tale of a married man's passion for a single girl. When she was questioned about the book, Marie replied that Dr. McDow had given her the novel and a gold watch. She was asked if her relationship with McDow was similar to that of the principals in the book.

"Non! In the book an unmarried woman loves a married man. It was not the case for me. I love him not!"

Marie also testified that Dr. McDow had told her he had married his German wife for her money, but that he didn't want to live with his wife anymore. He wanted Marie to leave Charleston with him, but she would not go.

The defendant took the stand on the third day of the trial. He spoke smoothly, except when he recounted the shooting. His voice broke as he tried to explain how Captain Dawson came flying into his office, expecting to find Marie submitting to his advances. "Captain Dawson was waving his cane in the air, and he struck me a glancing blow with the cane." The defense maintained that the doctor was merely protecting himself from further blows when he shot Captain Dawson.

On Saturday, the closing day of the trial, Major Julian Mitchell delivered the closing argument for the state. Before the jury left to deliberate on the defendant's innocence or guilt, they asked for a diagram of Dr. McDow's office. They left the courtroom for the deliberation.

Two hours later, the jury filed into the courtroom. Every eye was on them to see if their faces revealed any sign of their decision. There was none. The question everyone was waiting for was asked: "Has the jury reached a decision?"

"We find the defendant *not guilty*."

A hush came over the big, high-ceilinged room. Even the judge seemed stunned. The jury had deliberated for less than two hours. Almost everyone had believed the black jurors would insist on Dr. McDow's guilt. However, they had done the opposite. Many people felt that the verdict had not been a true one. They believed a love triangle had ended in murder when the doctor shot his rival in a jealous rage.

All quibbling about the verdict was abruptly silenced later that summer when Dr. McDow's body was found at his home on Rutledge Street. The death came during a hot spell, and days passed before the decomposed remains were discovered. Ever since that time, it has been said that the McDow house is haunted.

Bad Seed: The Murdering Bighams

I know 'um well enough to tell . . . them Bigham could talk like angel, but best you mind out—they have they own way of doing thing. Scared of Bigham.

Diana "Di" Shubrick

The year was 1909, and the striking young woman sitting at the kitchen table was horror-stricken. Her husband and his family were asking her to join them in their coverup of a murder. In fact, she and her husband had been called to this family conference in Pamplico from their home in Murrells Inlet to discuss this very matter. The trial was in a few weeks, and they were planning their testimony. The proud young woman sat quietly, trying to maintain her composure as she faced the seven of them—her husband, his mother, two brothers, two sisters, and sister-in-law.

"Well? Are you going along with us or not?" her husband barked.

Ruth raised her head but did not look at him. She was thinking there was no simple solution. The murder hadn't been clueless, but it came close to being motiveless. Smiley's temper was the cause of this terrible crime, just as it had been on other occasions of violence. Come to think of it, there was always some sort of deception going on because of Smiley and Edmund, and like his sisters and his mother, Cleve was always concealing their deviltry.

Ruth's eyes slowly moved to her husband, Dr. Grover Cleveland Bigham. Cleve wasn't filled out like his brothers. One might say he looked delicate. She saw that he had opened his coat and was pulling his suspenders out and letting them pop back against him, a sure sign that he was losing control. His normally professional poise had slipped a notch or two. At this moment he appeared to be anything but a well-educated physician. A thought suddenly hit her: Cleve's family was pulling him down to their level. Hadn't her family, the Crisps of Laurens County, South Carolina, warned her of such happenings? A worried look crossed her face. No one in her family had wanted her to marry Dr. Cleve Bigham. Her cousin was especially against it and warned, in a string of cliches, that it would be a disaster. "Birds of a feather flock together," she'd said. "Like father, like son. A chip off the old block." Nearly everyone in South Carolina knew that there had been murderers in the last two generations of Bighams. But following one's heart was easier than following one's head.

Cleve walked across the linoleum floor. It was a small, intimate room. The frame walls needed paint, but you didn't notice it so much since they were obscured by the cookstove, kitchen cabinet, icebox, and shelves cluttered with dishes and glassware. A coffee grinder was attached to a wall. Although most kitchens in the area were similar, few neighbors had visited this one to know what it looked like. Bigham acquaintances were few and far between. Friends were even rarer.

"This concerns all of us," Cleve said, lighting a cigarette. He took a few draws and flicked the cigarette with a finger, loosening ash which dropped into a cup on the table. "You *have* to go along with it. I give the orders around here." He crushed the cigarette into the cup and yanked off his coat and threw it on a chair.

Ruth's glance moved to Smiley. She trembled.

"Your indecision is a source of weakness," Smiley snapped. "If you go along with us, well that's one thing. But if you don't, well then, I don't know what we'd all think about that. It would weaken the stand I'm taking. The police are on my tail right now." He hit the table with his fist, and the cup holding Cleve's crumpled cigarette bounced. Ruth jumped. "You know what you've got to do. What to say, when you're asked. You're to say that I didn't leave this house that day, and you'd better damn well say that!"

"Suppose I prefer to, uh, take no part in this?" Ruth asked, her eyes lowering to the table. As she fingered a design in the cross-stitched tablecloth, she boldly went a step further. "What if I expose you, Smiley?" Her eyelids raised just enough to study Smiley's reaction.

"You don't have that option," Edmund cut in quickly. "You made your choice when you married Cleve. You're a part of this family, and you'll stick with us. Just tell the law that Smiley was right here all that day and that night, too."

Ruth ignored the remark. "Edmund and Smiley can't keep killing and getting away with it. Other people just don't act like that," she pleaded to the other family members.

"Well listen to the little well-bred snob," Edmund snarled. "Boy! She's something, isn't she?" He turned to his youngest brother. "Cleve, I'm glad she's yours and not mine."

Dora, the boys' mother, in whose house such family conferences took place, stirred. "You'd better think this over, girl. Don't make a mistake."

Dr. Cleve scowled, grabbed up his coat, and flung himself into the chair. Looking at his wife, he said soberly, "You already know what I'm about to say. But I'll make it crystal clear for your benefit. In South Carolina families are close. They've always been so. There is a union and fellowship that arises from common responsibilities and interests. There may be an occasional disagreement or argument, but no member is afforded the luxury of taking a stand against another. Like the Chinese, we aren't just a heap of loose sand; we're a unit. We're *family*." He paused, evaluated Ruth's facial expression, then summed it up with, "Well, how do we stand?"

"It seems to me that we're kind of like a jury," Edmund's wife May spoke up for the first time.

"Edmund," Ruth said, getting riled up, "May always takes up for you." Her eyes shot to Smiley. "Too bad you never married. Otherwise you'd have a wife to stick up for you, too."

"Why don't we just go around the room," May went on, ignoring Ruth's outburst, "and ask everybody what they'll say when the case comes up in court?"

"Good idea," Dr. Cleve said, stretching out his legs. "We'll poll the jury. Smiley, why don't you just ask us all?"

Smiley looked at his mother, but before he had time to ask her how she was voting, she said, "Son, I'm with you. You were here in this house all day on the day of Sam Johnson's murder in July. Neither of us left the house that day."

Smiley's eyes moved to his two sisters, who had been silently standing in the doorway. Both Leitha and Marjorie nodded in agreement. Leitha and Marjorie were pretty girls. They were frequently called "the *nice* Bighams." Had their fate been not to have been born Bighams, they would have been the village darlings. They were both married now and had moved away from the old homestead. Their husbands had been left at home; they couldn't be trusted with clan secrets.

Smiley's eyes moved to May.

"The Bigham luck has lasted for generations, and it must continue. Count me among the faithful," she chorused.

"Now. Ruth it's up to you," her husband said. "All the rest of us are accounted for. What do you say?"

At first Ruth hesitated. She started to speak, but then seemed to withdraw. Again she seemed ready to make a caustic remark, then coughed into her hand.

"Well? Come on out with it!" Cleve admonished.

"Perhaps you've all read the Book of Exodus," she said softly, her eyes searching the expressions of the others. "The Ten Commandments were given to Moses."

"We know what the Ten Commandments say," Smiley wisecracked. "It's what *you'll* say that we're waiting to hear."

"You can't make me do it!" Ruth screamed. Then she began to talk and went on until she was nearly hysterical. "Smiley was in a huff that day. Hotheaded. Oh, it was awful. I begged him not to go to the Johnson house while he was upset. I knew just as surely as I know that my name's Ruth that if he left the house there'd be another murder. I *knew* it." She sucked in her breath, wondering if she'd gone too far. She went further. "And you, Edmund, you were a part of it. That's for sure. For all I know, *you* could have driven that nail. But May will alibi for you 'til doomsday." Ruth's eyes, blinking as they moved around the room, quizzed the others. She saw only cold stares looking back. She felt trapped and her face mirrored her fear and desolation. There was a tiny quiver in her white neck. "In the courtroom in Florence they'll ask me to kiss the Bible and tell the truth. And you're asking me to kiss the Bible and tell a lie!"

Dr. Cleve ordered his wife out of the room. Ruth flew from the kitchen and up the stairs, leaving the hushed room behind her. Finally, Dr. Cleve spoke, his eyes sweeping the room. "Like it was with the ancient Greeks, there's a matter of family honor. You have my word for it. Ruth may not testify *for* Smiley, but she won't testify *against* him." He paused, wondering how to extricate Ruth. "She may not testify *at all.*"

For a moment no one spoke, and Cleve went into a reflective mood. During the argument he had become aware of so many things, not only about himself but about all of the Bighams. They were so like Grand-father Leonard. Leonard had founded the Bigham family fortune on two principles—the acquisition of land and family loyalty. The land came first. All of the Bighams who came after Grandfather Leonard had inherited his traits, the love of land and loyalty to family. It brought forth in them the same intense passion that evoked greed and lust for power in others.

For a moment, Cleve was forced back to the present when Smiley declared the conference was finished and the family dispersed. Then he settled back and was lost in the stories he'd heard as a child, and in his own memories.

Land was more than a passion to Leonard Bigham. It was an appe-tite. Truly, he was a driven man, always a little hungry. The smell of the pine trees on his property was an intoxicating perfume. He couldn't buy enough pineland, and what he bought, he protected. Driven by his in-tense love for his land, he became an insensitive man. But most of all, he became a feared man.

Leonard was bullheaded, with no regard for human life. Only such a person could carry out the deranged plan for raising a family which Leonard devised. With his iron-willed determination, Leonard set in motion his plan to teach his children how to survive and succeed in life. The plan was to teach them how to murder without getting caught!

Leonard secretly instructed his children, and he soon realized that Leonard Smiley, Jr., known as Smiley, was his most adept child. Washington was too slow, and Mary Margaret—as a girl—would never rule the Bigham clan. But Leonard never had to explain anything twice to Smiley, even when he gave instructions on murder. He had taught his children there were two kinds of murders: clean and messy. When the day came that Leonard was to demonstrate a clean murder, he chose a dog named Trial. "I musta known this stubborn animal woulda come to a bad end when I named him Trial," Leonard quipped, as he began his lesson.

From the kitchen to the stableyard he brought a bowl of table scraps that included chicken bones, sweet potato pie, and cornmeal mush. Leonard removed a tiny bottle from his pocket. Trial, licking his lips, raised his front paws and rested them on Leonard's knees. "See?" Leonard focused his attention on Smiley. "Trial just can't wait to get his dinner. What he doesn't know is that this'll be his *last* dinner." The children's eyes were wide as their father poured some crystals in the scraps of leftover dinner. "This here's crystals of potassium cyanide. Now just you watch what happens when this hound laps it up."

Leonard put the bowl on the ground. Just as he had predicted, Trial gobbled it hungrily. A few seconds after that, the dog tried to walk away, but his hind legs wouldn't support him. Trial dragged himself a short distance, putting his weight on his front legs. Tears came to his eyes, and he shook his head as though a bee were on his nose. Suddenly, he fell to the ground. There was a slight attempt to stand up, but all four legs now failed the animal. As Trial went down for the last time, he was looking at Leonard. His tail wagged twice, then he went limp. According to Leonard, this was a clean murder.

The demented father selected a hot summer day to exhibit a messy murder for his children's education. There was a man who lived on the farm whom everyone called Small, due to his slight stature. Leonard carried a grudge against Small because he felt the man was all but useless as a farm worker. Small couldn't be counted on to work when timber was being cut and hauled away since he was not a man of great strength. To make matters worse, Small was intelligent, and Leonard believed the man was suspicious of some of his theories and practices. If one man had to go, this was the one. Besides, his wife would be afraid to make trouble.

The night before, not long after midnight, a savage storm had struck Leonard's farm. The wind blew and rattled the windows and howled down the chimney. Then came the deluge. Sheets of rain smashed against the house and turned the yard into random streams of mud. The sky was aroar with rolling peals of thunder, each overlapping another, like cannon fire in a war.

On the morning of the murder, Leonard and his children walked through the forest to examine the pines. Leonard had grown up amid the wild storms of the South Carolina Low Country, but when a storm destroyed one of his pine trees, he usually went beserk with rage. He couldn't stand to lose his fine pines to anything other than the axe of a lumberjack, but sometimes one bolt of lightning would hit as many as four of Leonard's tall trees. But Leonard wasn't angry today; one of his fallen pines was going to be used in a valuable lesson. When they came upon a huge tree that had been split down the middle by lightning, Leonard had the children sit on the ground and wait for him.

Sometime later he returned, and Small was with him. As Small stood looking at the damaged tree, Leonard struck him at the base of the skull and knocked him out. The unconscious man was pulled to the base of the disfigured tree, and Leonard took a rag from his pocket and smothered him. Later, when Small was found by friends, they believed he had been hit by lightning. Small was buried, and his wife had a grave marker placed at the head of the burial mound. The crude wooden monument had been chiseled in the likeness of a man, with a zigzag bolt of lightning striking him in the chest. This had been a messy murder, Leonard told his children.

Years passed, and the lessons continued, with special emphasis on how to manipulate the law to get what you wanted. Three generations of Bighams had amassed 2,500 acres, creating an isolated kingdom of their own. Leonard wanted to make sure his progeny knew that Bigham law could triumph over civil law.

Then Leonard unexpectedly found himself accused of one of his "messy murders." He faced his accuser across the Marion County courtroom.

Mindy Jackson, drawn up like a scared animal, cringed in the courtroom chair and wondered where she'd gotten the courage to sign the warrant which had brought Leonard Bigham to court. Everyone knew the wealthy, intimidating Bighams won every contest, one way or another. Mindy's case was a classic study in futility.

"You are charged with the murder of William Jackson," Solicitor Shaw said. "What say you, Leonard Bigham?"

"Not guilty!" Leonard spoke with a confident, resonant voice, although he was a bit out of sorts. If he'd had any idea that Mindy would dare to bring him before the bar of justice, he'd have taken care of her, too. At the time he'd butchered her husband, that rascal William, he could just as easily have killed her and shut her mouth forever. But the last thing in the world he'd ever have believed was that Mindy would swear out a warrant for his arrest. William had deserved what he got. The nerve of that man, refusing to chop the cotton after sundown. Those niggers could see 'til slap dark. Oh well, for his refusal to continue working in the field, he'd gotten his due. And in time, Mindy would get hers.

To Leonard this trial was simply an untidy piece of legal procedure. But to those who sat in scattered knots in the courtroom, it was more. It was unsettling to think how frequently Leonard Bigham killed, with little or no provocation. As always, the case against him seemed too hazy and contradictory to convict him.

As she sat before the judge, Mindy's mind could still picture her dying husband in his last moments. Leonard Bigham had called to William to come outside his cabin. Hearing that harsh and boisterous voice, William stepped into his britches. Just as William closed the screen door behind him, Leonard shouted profane words, and a volley of shots exploded. When Mindy ran out the door, William's watery, weak eyes begged for help. He was lying on the ground, and blood was pouring into the sand. Leonard Bigham was on the sorrel mare that was galloping into the darkness.

When the time came for the defense to present its case, Mindy straightened up and listened intently. One major question arose. How could Leonard be in two places at the same time? Every family member had testified—very convincingly—that Leonard Bigham hadn't left home on the night of William Jackson's murder.

Mindy realized that all she had feared was coming true. A black girl like her was condemned by birth to a life of poverty and injustice. Life was a violent and vicious class struggle, and justice didn't stand a chance.

The jury deliberated only ten minutes on the case of the black servant versus the wealthy and influential Bigham. In bold script, "Not guilty" was scribbled on the back of the indictment.

The Bigham children had learned another lesson: you could even be accused of murder and stand trial, and still get away with it.

For a while these lessons lay dormant, but when Smiley Bigham, Jr., was thirty, he was overcome with desire for power of the kind his father possessed. After all, Leonard was a rich man. His personal assets included thirty miles of pineland bordering the Great Pee Dee River. It also occurred to the son that he wouldn't have control over anything as long as his father lived. The more he thought about it, the more his fantasies took control of his mind. Gradually, he became more and more frustrated by his father's position of authority. Leonard was their figurehead, their totem. Leonard distanced himself from them, yet controlled them, and Smiley had had enough of it.

Smiley thought back over his training and pictured his father dropping dead from a meal of mush containing crystals of potassium cyanide. Mindy Jackson still cooked for the family, and if death came soon after the cyanide was injested by the stomach, wouldn't the public believe that Mindy had finally gotten retribution for the death of her husband? Besides that, murder by poisoning was one of the hardest things in the book to prove. Leonard himself had said that. Smiley carefully made his plans, working out a scheme to establish himself as the new figurehead of the family. He had learned his lessons well, and no finger of accusation was pointed at him.

On the day Leonard Bigham died, word quickly spread over the countryside. The sudden death was a mystery, but rumor had it that the man had been poisoned. When a few acquaintances came to the Bigham house to express their condolences, Smiley was outwardly disconsolate. Two days later, when Leonard's remains were lowered into the grave, Smiley broke down.

Rumors persisted. Had Mindy poisoned Leonard? Everyone wanted to know, but they also agreed that if she had, she certainly had a good reason. Indeed, no one would have blamed her.

An investigator was appointed, but he was never able to put together a conclusive case against anyone. No one urged him to use other resources in trying to determine what brought Leonard down. No one seemed to care. A driven and dreaded man was at rest. Curiosity over the event finally waned, and Smiley was pleased when the talk died down. He was ready to get on with his life.

Now that Smiley considered himself head of the family, he realized that he should have his own house. As he thought about it, not just any house would be fitting; it would have to be special. A structure of two stories, situated on a hill with a view of the countryside, was what he pictured in his mind. He would make it clear to the builders that the new Bigham residence must be as everlasting as possible, and yet radiate a certain dignity.

Construction got under way, not too far from Smiley's mother's house. Workers were given a free hand at cutting all of the virgin pine trees necessary to build the residence. The sound of falling trees rang out through the forest day after day, and on some occasions work continued until after sunset.

When completed, the house was graceful and gave the precise effect Smiley had desired. One day as he stood in front and looked around, it came to him that the house needed a woman. *He needed a wife.* It would be pleasant to hear the clatter of china in the kitchen and to have someone to talk to by a winter's fire. Smiley looked around the area, but there was no one who met his requirements. His wife would have to be a strong woman who could carry her share of the load, as well as bear children. As he hadn't compromised on his house, neither would he compromise on his wife. He'd continue to look until he found the ideal helpmate. He had almost given up finding the perfect girl when he was introduced to Dora Smith of Greenville County. At first glance he knew he had found a wife.

Dora came into Smiley's life without a shred of information about the Bighams. It was clear they were wealthy, and there was no question that Smiley was a showoff, but other than that she knew little. Dora was only sixteen years old, and she showed little wisdom or maturity. Instead of taking her time to analyze the situation and get to know Smiley, she agreed to an immediate marriage. Dora used equally little wisdom in the first days of her marriage. She shrieked and screamed when angered, and Smiley returned the emotion with full measure. One day they were at it hot and heavy.

"I dare you to strangle me!" Dora shouted. "Just try it."

"I paid your pa a fat ransom for you," Smiley shouted, "and you're not worth a penny." He shook his head. "I've been cheated."

"You've been cheated? What about me? Do you think I like to be screamed at, pushed around, bruised, and scraped? You've got another think coming if you think I like what *I* got!"

As the days went by, Dora found her husband's domination increasingly abhorrent, and she rebelled, something that took Smiley by surprise. He decided to lighten up on Dora and give her a chance to get used to him and his ways, for he still believed she could be "fashioned into a good wife" for him. She was tough and could do strenuous work, and he had noted a mean streak in her. That was an asset. She could turn out to be the best investment he'd ever made, but he would have to be patient as he helped her find her true place in his life. Besides, the hairsplitting arguments were sapping his energy.

Dora didn't change until Smiley did. Now when he felt a slow rage boiling up within him, he stopped it immediately and became tender with his wife. This new personality was a piece of theater, unreal, but Dora began to fall for the act. She wondered what had been wrong with her. Smiley was courteous and agreeable, and when he became otherwise, it was probably her fault. She was little more than a child, and she had come into the marriage knowing nothing of what was expected of her. She decided she hadn't made the slightest effort to be agreeable.

Dora was soon expecting one child and talking of having another, as she wanted several children. Smiley swore any children he had would be "true" Bighams. His father had taught by example, and Smiley believed his father's teachings had been perfect. After all, the Bighams had always gotten away with their crimes. Surely they had done something right to break every law of the land and never spend a night in jail. Their success couldn't be improved upon—or could it?

As Smiley, Jr., deliberated on his family's past, it occurred to him that the Bighams had learned the law, had broken the law, but they had never *made* the law. Wouldn't that be the most challenging thing? He could acquire a fortune. Everything he had ever dreamed of would be in the palm of his hand if he could win a seat in the South Carolina House of Representatives. He swore to do it, even if it killed him.

Smiley lived near Florence, although his house was just over the county line in Marion County. When he ran for the right to represent Marion County in the House of Representatives, he was almost as surprised as everyone else in the county when he learned he had won the election. If only his father Leonard could see him now, he thought. A Bigham would actually be making the laws!

For a while there was a honeymoon period between Smiley and the voters of his district. He spoke eloquently before the House on subjects close to the hearts of his constituents. He voted in favor of legislation that concerned fishing and seining in Low Country waters, and he addressed the reduction of the expenses of government. When Smiley's first term was completed, in the eyes of his constituents, he was a prominent citizen.

With one term as a congressman behind him, Smiley began to dream of new heights. When the time was right, he announced his intentions to seek the office of senator from Marion County. But this time, Smiley was defeated, and he detested the feeling of being whipped. No Bigham was about to acquiesce to a setback. They were winners, and masters of the game, every game. As luck would have it, soon after his defeat the portion of Marion County in which Smiley lived was formed into a new county, Florence County. Smiley ran for the office of senator for the new county, and this time he won the election.

"My star is rising, Dora," he said proudly.

"Well, your star doesn't have much farther to go," she answered. "You're already higher than anybody around here gets."

"I don't want you to call me Smiley anymore. Call me 'Senator Bigham,' or you can call me 'the senator' when talking with others. I'm going to buy a top hat. That's how the people who were good enough to vote for me will see me. Arriving at my office in a top hat!"

"Why don't you grow a beard?" Dora's eyes sparked fierce interest as she gazed at her husband.

Aware that he had now captured Dora's complete attention, Smiley spoke excitedly. "Absolutely. A beard would be perfect for the image I want to project. Say, Dora, I like that idea of yours."

Smiley used his role of senator to the fullest degree, and it wasn't long before he believed he'd reached the pinnacle of promoting himself. But as always, when he reached his goal, and no new challenge was revealed, he began to lose interest.

Smiley's inattention and boredom with his job wasn't lost on the voters. The racy and colorful Senator Bigham, who always wore a top hat to his office, was now dull and contrary. His insolence annoyed those with whom he came into contact. Smiley declared that he wouldn't take time to campaign during the next election. He was anxious to pursue activities more to his liking and training. But, although he wasn't aware of it at the time, Leonard Smiley Bigham, Jr., was not invincible. Although he was sure everyone would vote for him, the people vividly remembered how he had lost interest in the job once he had mastered it, and they did not re-elect him.

Smiley became despondent, overtaken by melancholy, and his family had a difficult time just living in the same house with him. So engulfed was he by his hurt pride that he didn't speak to his family for weeks at a time. It was while he was in one of these dark moods that his favorite sharecropper, Lassus, came to him for his share of the money that was due from three bales of cotton he had produced. An argument arose when Smiley said that Lassus shared only in the profits from two of the three bales. When Smiley lunged at him, Lassus ran home. In a towering rage, Smiley loaded his rifle, then put a pistol in his pocket. He then walked deliberately over to the sharecropper's cabin and banged on the door. When no one answered, Smiley shifted the rifle from his shoulder to his arm and knocked again. Again, no answer. Smiley spread his legs apart, took aim, and shot through the door. The bullet went straight through the heart of Lassus. Before the authorities arrived, Smiley placed the pistol in the hand of the sharecropper. When the coroner arrived, Smiley told him that the killing had been in self-defense. The coroner believed Smiley.

Not long after this murder, Smiley's mother, who had been no match for her husband or Smiley, died. Smiley wept uncontrollably as the remains were lowered into the grave, but a few hours later he produced a will signed by his mother that no one else had ever seen. She had left all of her assets to him.

Getting his mother to leave him everything was the easiest thing in the world for Smiley. She had always listened to and followed every word her husband had said, and after his death Smiley was available to fill the vacuum. Anything Smiley, Jr., said was the law of the family.

Smiley did have two siblings, however. His brother, Washington, was no problem. Wash was so dimwitted he didn't even know or care what Smiley did. On the other hand, his sister, Mary Margaret, was a potential problem. She had married George Sanderson, a schoolteacher, and she was no fool.

Sure enough, Mary Margaret did take the case of her mother's estate to court, but Smiley won the lawsuit. Mary Margaret even appealed the case until it finally reached the state supreme court, but the decision of the lower court was upheld. She was just no match for Smiley.

Smiley took over his mother's house and forced Mary Margaret out at gunpoint. She and her husband moved to Marion. George's health was deteriorating, and he soon died. Mary Margaret, undernourished, broke, and disheartened over being cast aside by Smiley, took to the streets of Marion, begging for nickles and dimes. By the time she died, her brother Washington was also dead. After the deaths of his brother and sister, Smiley had no opposition to the inheritance left by his mother, and his assets amounted to more than $100,000.

Smiley next turned his attention to the education of his five children. He expected his two daughters to marry and leave home. But from the sons—Smiley III, Edmund, and Grover Cleveland—he expected *esprit de corps* and true Bigham traits.

Smiley planned to teach his children many things, but he decided they should first learn how to be cross-examined just in case they were ever taken to court. Each night after supper, following his father

Leonard's example, Smiley set up a mock court trial. The boys, aged eight to twelve, took turns as witnesses, and Smiley cross-examined each one relentlessly. If one erred in an answer, he was whipped.

Smiley soon decided to give his sons some real-life, on-the-spot training. He falsely accused a neighbor of stealing some of his hogs. During the trial, the boys—Smiley, Edmund, and Cleve—sat as still as death, taking all of it in. When the judge asked Smiley how he could identify his hogs, he replied that they had developed a peculiar twirl of their tails. Smiley stole a glance at his children to see if they were giving undivided attention to this show staged principally for their eyes. There wasn't as much as a murmur coming from them.

The court found judgment in favor of Smiley, and his neighbor was sentenced to pay a fine of one hundred dollars or spend ninety days at hard labor. Stealing a glance at the defendant, a smirk spread over Smiley's mouth. He then turned his attention to his boys. They were being well trained to fit into his plans for their lives; they had now learned how to manipulate the law. All three boys were clever and resourceful, cagey and calculating, and if one had more cunning than another, Smiley didn't know which one it was.

Leonard Smiley Bigham III, also known as Smiley like his father, was his mother's favorite. He was the oldest, and Dora saw no impropriety in siding with him in any debate. More and more, her husband became jealous of this relationship, and he began to abuse Dora physically because of his jealousy. But that still didn't stop her from favoring young Smiley or taking his side in anything he did. When he received his first shotgun, he promptly stepped off one hundred paces, turned, and slowly raised the gun, which was loaded with birdshot. When he pulled the trigger, the tiny shot went into the backside of a woman bending over a washtub. Her scream brought interest to Smiley's eyes. He was only fifteen.

Grover Cleveland Bigham, known as Cleve, was the youngest of the children. At the time of Cleve's birth, Smiley was running for the congressional seat, and he wanted his son to bear a prominent political name. From the beginning, Cleve was different. He took the time to develop his mind. He read books that were considered much too advanced for a boy of his age, and in order to read, he hid in trees, unused rooms, anywhere where he was likely not to be disturbed. At seventeen he was admitted to the medical school at the College of Charleston.

Edmund, the middle son, was said to be "the spittin' image" of

Grandfather Leonard. Like his grandfather, his hair was the color of ripe wheat, his forehead angular, and his eyes were gray and stormy. But the feature that was most Bigham-like was the subtle I've-got-something-on-you expression. Not only did he learn to intimidate the other children in the family, he soon mastered the technique of arching his eyebrows in mock innocence when he was suspected of being mixed up in anything distasteful. Once when a schoolteacher rebuked Edmund, the boy vowed revenge. The next morning the teacher went to the barn to harness his mare only to find the animal had been brutally attacked and was dying. Marjorie, one of Edmund's two sisters, whispered to her father that Edmund had jabbed a pitchfork into the mare's side, over and over again. Upon hearing this, her father raised his chest and squared his shoulders. Edmund was a Bigham all right. Yes sirree. All three were real smart boys.

As time went on, the neighbors became aware that Edmund was becoming an expert marksman. The boy would stick five straws into a bale of cotton, count one hundred paces, turn, and in five shots cut each straw in half. This achievement gained Edmund a new prestige, and it soon became apparent that he was obsessed with guns.

As the children matured, they all showed evidence of ambition. Smiley, Jr., soon became suspicious of their goals. His sons didn't level with him anymore, and he didn't feel right about it. He, of all people, realized the risks and consequences of what he had created. His big face became haggard and drawn. As hard as he tried to choke back his suspicions, they wouldn't be smothered. Finally, Smiley became so afraid, he would eat only food that Dora cooked. Smiley was twenty years older than Dora, but he looked and felt even older than his years. Even Dora's culinary talents couldn't put much weight on his frame. One day someone whispered to Smiley that he had heard a member of his family say he would be glad to be rid of the "crazy old fool." Someone else reported that his daughter was overheard saying, "Dad is mad."

Ironically, death came to Leonard Smiley Bigham, Jr., just as it had to his father. He was poisoned in May 1908. After the burial, some people gossiped about the cause of death, but nobody seemed to really care. By now it was an accepted fact that the Bigham men were fed poison when the other family members deemed it necessary.

By the time of their father's death, all three of the boys were settling into adulthood. Edmund had chosen a wife. May was not particularly exciting, in fact she was rather dull, but Edmund realized that with proper handling she would lose her archaic ideas of conduct and become manageable. Looks and excitement May would never have, but she wouldn't be hard to change or to spend a life with, particulary since she was infatuated with the Bigham wealth.

Cleve had also married, but Smiley III could never find a suitable wife. He didn't fit into the mold of a family man and everyone knew it. As he began to take over his father's personal matters, riding his father's favorite mount around the farm, sibling jealousy arose between Smiley and Edmund. When Edmund questioned his authority, Smiley explained that his mother had put him in charge of his father's affairs, and he claimed that with Edmund working in a garage, *someone* had to take charge. To pacify Edmund, Smiley gave him a small farm on which Edmund built a house of concrete blocks. Although bitterness was building between the two brothers, the solidarity of the Bigham family was still intact.

Everything was going smoothly for the Bighams until late one afternoon on a July day in 1909. Sunlight filtered through the trees lining the path to the stableyard. Two men in straw hats, wet with perspiration that caused their shirts to cling to their backs, led mules to the barn. One of the animals had suffered an eye injury. Smiley, sitting on the porch of the house, saw the mule, jumped up and ran to meet them.

"What happened to the mule?" Smiley demanded.

"Sam threw dirt in its eye. But, lissen Mr. Smiley, that mule just wouldn't budge." It was clear that Jack Dooley was frightened of mean-tempered Smiley.

Smiley's eyes narrowed. "Sam, you threw sand in the mule's eye?"

"Mr. Smiley, I didn't mean to. You see, that mule wouldn't go. I tried to move him, but I couldn't."

"How old are you?" Smiley asked.

"Seventeen."

Smiley's jaw sagged. "As old as that and you don't know how to treat a mule!"

"Yes, sir, I know how to treat a mule, but that stubborn thing just stood there like an idiot."

Anger flooded Smiley's face. "I can always get a man to work for me, but I can't always get a good mule," he said slowly and deliberately.

"Mr. Smiley," Sam began, "I didn't mean to—"

At that moment, Smiley picked up a bucket and threw it at Sam. The bucket missed its target, and Sam took off, running as fast as he could toward the cabin where he lived with his mother.

The following morning Sam didn't report to work at the Bigham farm. Smiley went over to the Johnson house and demanded to talk to Sam, but the boy's mother said he was working in Pamplico, several miles up the road. She told him Sam wouldn't be working for him anymore; she wouldn't permit it. In a fit of anger, Smiley left the Johnson house. It was evident he was consumed with rage. How dare the little upstart refuse to work for him? As he threw a leg over his mount, the boy's mother pleaded with him to keep peace and not harm her son.

Smiley went home. Soon after he got there, Cleve's wife Ruth arrived at the door for a visit.

"It's good to see you, Smiley," she said sweetly.

"Come in," Smiley scowled.

Ruth stepped into the front hall and smoothed the skirt of her dress. She was delicate and lovely, but her appearance did nothing to soothe Smiley's mood. It was at once apparent to her that she was confronting an unquestionably irritable and surly man. Still, displaying an innate sense of social grace, Ruth remarked on the heat of the day and the journey she had endured. Smiley stared down at her. "Well, what did you expect? Just to leave your house and arrive here by magic?"

"My, Smiley, but you are grouchy today," Ruth answered. "Are you in any sort of trouble?"

"What's it to you?"

"I'm worried about you."

"You don't need to worry about me."

Ruth walked toward the parlor, and Smiley followed, keeping a watchful eye on her. As they sat in the parlor, it was considerably cooler, but a silence developed between them.

Ruth grasped an opportunity to break the silence. "Nice, isn't it? The parlor, I mean. So cool."

"Absolutely," Smiley answered, his voice going down an octave and becoming grouchier.

Ruth again asked Smiley what was the matter.

He looked around the room helplessly, his face white and tense. And then he began to talk about what had happened, how Sam Johnson had thrown sand into his mule's eye.

"Oh, come on, Smiley," Ruth bantered. "Don't get so excited. Nothing's so terrible about that. Sam's temper just got the best of him for a moment."

Smiley glared at Ruth in astonishment. She had a flair for making his actions sound dogmatic, silly, and impulsive. It maddened him. A tightness grabbed his chest. He decided she was underestimating the situation. His anger accelerated as he thought how much he detested her uppity Laurens County purity. He began to unbraid her for her stupidity.

Ruth was surprised by Smiley's reaction. She regarded him sharply, but said in a calm tone, "There's no need to fly off the handle."

As Smiley's facial muscles became tighter and more intense, Ruth begged him to forget the incident and calm down. But her words fell on deaf ears.

"I'm going to load my Winchester," Smiley spat, "and get this matter over with right now."

Ruth sat perfectly still, gripped in fear. A sudden tremor swept through her. What was Smiley going to do? It would surely be something headstrong and wild. She closed her eyes, disgusted, squeamish. After a few moments, she opened her eyes. Going to a window she saw Smiley on his horse. He had his Winchester. She watched as he rode across the road. He seemed to be heading toward Edmund's house, and that puzzled her. After all she had just heard, she thought he'd go straight to the Johnson cabin.

By the time Smiley arrived at Sam Johnson's house, other men were with him. Each man carried a gun. Smiley kicked open the door and marched inside the cabin, his henchmen following behind. They searched the cabin. Sam, his mind stuck in neutral, lay frozen under a bed. Smiley stooped down, clamped a hand around Sam's wrist, and pulled him out.

"It won't do you no good to kill me," Sam cried. "The law will find out."

"I must say," Smiley growled, "there are several things to take into account in planning a killing. But the law is not one of them. They're all knotheads." With the barrel of his gun at Sam's back, Smiley walked him out of the house.

The party of men rode to a boggy swamp, stagnant and thick with briars, thorns, and overhanging vines. Smiley pulled Sam from the horse and threw him on the ground. He then grabbed Sam around the ankles. The boy squirmed frantically to free himself. While Smiley held Sam by the ankles, the other men began beating and kicking him. Sam's shrieks were loud and pitiful. Finally, he was knocked senseless, bleeding profusely. One of the men took a hammer and nail from his pocket. The nail was placed in the boy's ear and driven into his head until it reached the brain. No more sounds came from the victim, whose face now had the countenance of death.

The frail, distraught mother was already searching for her son. She crept among low-hanging limbs, pushed at thickets of briars, drug her scratched and bleeding feet through stagnant slime, and blew insects from the air around her face until the hunt finally ended around daylight when she found her son's bruised and swollen body in the bog. Running home, screaming, calling out to God to let her son be alive, she attracted the attention of a young man who, upon hearing her disjointed story, went for the law.

After arriving at the scene and making a preliminary examination, the coroner announced that the cause of death was from a loss of blood, probably caused by the scratches and cuts inflicted by the thorns and briars in the overhanging growth—and those induced by a heavy instrument. Just then he noticed a stain of blood near the boy's ear, and his eyes went to the nail head.

The sheriff was bent on finding the person or persons responsible for the savage murder. "I shall track down the perpetrator of this butchery," he vowed. He was in luck. Fresh hoof prints led the sheriff and the coroner straight to Edmund Bigham's concrete-block house. The sound of horses prancing to a stop startled Edmund. He jumped.

Outside, the coroner and sheriff sat on their horses, talking quietly. They agreed that no ordinary murderer would execute such a grisly death as this one. Not only was the murderer the most depraved of men, he was altogether inhuman in his actions. Such a crime could only have been motivated by revenge.

The men received a cordial welcome from Edmund and May. The officers were asked to have a seat, but the sheriff got right to the point and asked Edmund about the murder of Sam Johnson. Edmund looked shocked and said he hadn't heard anything about it.

May reached for a chair and eased herself into it. "I declare it can't be true," she drawled. She was wearing a pink voile dress with a full skirt, puffed sleeves, and a large, starched-stiff white collar. Although the frock was a little frayed and faded, its simplicity conveyed an impression of virtue and honesty. Most people considered May plain and simple, but the officers saw golden highlights in her honey-colored hair and softness and common sense in the innocent eyes. Why, she's a pillar of morality, and there's no question about it, the sheriff was thinking. "Edmund didn't leave this house," May assured the sheriff and coroner. "He was right here." The sheriff was convinced that Edmund and May were telling the truth.

The next stop was the home of Dora and Smiley. Although Smiley was adamant in declaring his innocence, the sheriff didn't believe him and arrested him for the murder of Sam Johnson. Two other men, Andy Fuller and Daniel Hinds, were also arrested. The three were taken to the cabin of Sam Johnson's mother, who looked them over carefully. Finally, she said she had not seen their faces on the night her son was taken, but that she was positive that Smiley Bigham was in the group. She would never forget the sound of his voice. The court case against the three men was docketed for October 1909 in Florence County Criminal Court.

Bond was posted for Smiley, and it was then that he called a family conference.

After the family conference, Ruth and Dr. Cleve returned to their home near Murrells Inlet. Both were angry.

"What do you want of me?" Dr. Cleve screamed. "To not give a damn? To exist without responsibility? Without family solidarity?"

Ruth, dizzy from the reaction to the solitary, comfortless course she had chosen, didn't answer. For the next three days, her husband refused to speak to her. She reflected over and over again on her husband's accusation, and she decided it was true up to a point. She wanted Cleve not to give a damn about Smiley and Edmund. Obviously they had inherited the murderous traits of their father and grandfather. But Cleve had always been called the brainy, artistic one. It would never occur to him, she believed, to kill anyone. Although he frequently overlooked the dishonesty and immorality of his brothers, all of Cleve's medical training had taught him to promote health, improve it, prolong it. But Ruth underestimated his family's influence on Cleve—and his early training.

One day, without any real resolution of their differences, Ruth and Cleve began to communicate again. Later in the day, Mr. and Mrs. William Avant arrived for a visit, and Ruth heated a kettle of water for tea. As they sipped tea and chatted over the porcelain cups, the Avants invited Ruth and Cleve to be their guests at Sunnyside, the Avant home in Murrells Inlet. Aside from being one of the most outstanding houses in the coastal region, Sunnyside was also located on one of the most spectacular sites. It stood on a bluff by a creek which meandered through the marshlands. (Across the marsh was a sliver of sand that would one day become Garden City Beach.)

Quickly, Dr. Cleve and Ruth accepted the Avants' invitation. Ruth especially viewed the visit with eagerness, for she so adored the stairway made of solid mahogany that wound from the first floor to the attic, and the wide hallway which ran through the center of the house, with its high ceiling and generous proportions. But the thing Ruth loved most about visiting the Avants at Sunnyside was that she could take an evening dip in the creek. Nothing satisfied or thrilled her more than slipping into her bathing attire, throwing her white raincoat over her shoulders, and skipping down to the creek, especially if there happened to be a moon that night. Just the thought of sliding into the cool water made her shiver.

But Dr. Cleve was viewing the invitation in quite a different way. He knew William Avant was a man who could be easily manipulated, especially when he'd had a glass or two of bourbon. He was highly respected, and all of that, particularly as the owner of Sunnyside, but he also believed in many customs, practices, and legends that had their roots in Africa. Murrells Inlet was located in the plantation area where dozens of descendants of slaves still practiced the old-time beliefs and customs. The influence of the former slaves was not lost on the whites who lived in this area. Many a well-educated, aristocratic white was as superstitious as the descendants of the African slaves. It was firmly believed by many of the area's residents that five types of varmints roamed the Murrells Inlet woods: plat-eyes, boo-daddies, hants, hags, and ghosts. Ghosts were the most feared of all.

At first, Dr. Cleve hadn't been interested in the invitation, but the more he thought about it, the more it seemed the perfect solution. He knew Ruth would leave the house about dusk, and as she pranced and cavorted her way to the creek in her white raincoat, she *could* be mistaken for a ghost. Especially by Avant, if he happened to be sitting on the porch after consuming several glasses of bourbon. Everyone who knew Avant knew he had a phobia about ghosts, and he would take any action necessary to prevent one from coming onto his property. As Cleve formulated his plan, he believed that it was so simple it was amusing.

Dr. Cleve told Ruth to be sure to pack her bathing clothing for their visit to Sunnyside. Among the things he had packed for himself were three bottles of Avant's favorite brand of bourbon and his own pistol.

The next day as Ruth was packing for the visit, another drama was taking place at Edmund's house.

"Get our things packed," Edmund snapped to May. "With Smiley's trial coming up, things are too hot here right now. We're getting out and leaving no tracks behind."

"But, we promised to testify—"

"Shut up! Do as you're told. We're skipping this place," Edmund shouted.

May soon had the belongings packed. She dressed Eloise, their little girl, and told Edmund they were ready to go.

"We'll go to south Georgia," Edmund said hurriedly. "I'll sell this house when we get settled there."

Late that same afternoon, Dr. Cleve and Ruth arrived at Sunnyside. Ruth was worried about Cleve. He had shown little patience with her that day, and he seemed nervous and preoccupied. As they made their way to Sunnyside, Ruth's mind was racing as she tried to figure out what he was up to, if anything. Instinct told her that *something* was up, and she was scared.

Mrs. Avant met them at the door, her face full of charm. Ruth's taut body relaxed and she told herself she had been imagining things. She glanced around as she stepped into one of her favorite homes. Cleve and Mr. Avant went upstairs as Ruth went to a window where she had a view of the creek. The sun was already seeping into the oaks and pines, hazing them into a golden blush, and Ruth knew that the night would be perfect. She was thankful that Cleve had carried her grip and raincoat upstairs, giving her this short reverie. The very moment when the sun sinks into the west, and the transformation of day into twilight takes place, is a time to be savored, Ruth thought.

Upstairs, Cleve placed his grip in the armoire and set Ruth's on a small cot at the foot of the high-poster bed. He threw her white raincoat on her grip and took the time to sit for a moment on the cot. Avant left the room, saying that Cleve had time for a nap before supper. The idea of a short nap appealed to Cleve, whose nerves had almost gotten the best of him. He removed Ruth's grip and raincoat and stretched out on the cot. It wasn't unusual for such a bunk to be located at the foot of a large bed. They once had been used for women in childbirth; a midwife could sit on the floor and easily assist the woman on the cot. Now the cots were most frequently used for naps.

"Oh, isn't it all just too marvelous?" Ruth remarked a little later as she came into the bedroom.

Cleve jumped off the cot instantly, coming out of a deep sleep. "Yes," he answered, still a little disoriented. After getting up and rubbing his eyes, he put Ruth's grip and raincoat back on the cot.

Ruth observed her husband and thought how very much he needed this reprieve from his medical practice and family problems. The business about Smiley, and her unwillingness to go along with the deception, obviously still rankled him. But she hoped he harbored no grudges.

"It *is* splendid being here," she said. "I'm looking forward to my dip in the creek after supper."

"I hope you enjoy it," Cleve said, reminding himself that he must not upset Ruth unduly. Not now when within hours she was to suffer a terrible, uh, shock. Cleve suddenly adopted a merriment he did not feel. "You must also take a stroll along the shore."

Ruth thought about that remark. She didn't know what he meant. Of course she'd walk along the shore, but why was her husband suddenly so interested in her evening swim? She pondered this new development as she went downstairs. Mrs. Avant was setting the table for supper, and Ruth asked if she could help.

"Yes," Mrs. Avant replied. "You may take the ice pick and chip some ice for the glasses on the table."

Ruth took each glass to the big wooden icebox, and as she chipped ice from a large block in the metal-lined cabinet, her husband walked into the kitchen.

"What's up?" Cleve asked.

"I'm filling the glasses with ice," Ruth answered. "Dinner is just about ready, dear."

After Ruth put the glasses back on the table, Mrs. Avant poured tea from a pitcher. Cleve sat down at the table just as Avant came in, carrying a platter of fried fish.

"Never have any trouble getting fresh fish around here," Avant said. "Someone's always fishing and sharing."

As the meal got under way, there was a wonderful feeling of goodfellowship in the air, with much friendly bantering rising above the clack-clack, swish-swish of the small boats plying the water in the creek not far from the house. Cleve, unnoticed by the others, was keeping a watchful eye on Ruth. He was preoccupied, that he never once noticed the love for the Avants and for Sunnyside which showed in her eyes. Her face was virtually glowing with wonderment and excitement.

As they dined, Mr. Avant launched into the history of Murrells Inlet—tales of pirates who had buried their loot there, of hurricanes and wars, and superstitions about creatures in the woodlands. Ruth loved it all. She could have listened to him go on and on. The two of them shared a love for this ancient South Carolina village under the oaks, on the creek so near the sea. But Mrs. Avant glanced at the clock and said that if Ruth was to enjoy her swim in the creek, they must suspend the storytelling until later.

"Yes," Cleve added. "Ruth, go upstairs and get into your bathing suit and raincoat."

"Mrs. Avant, can't I help with the dishes?"

"No. You run along now. I'll take care of the dishes."

Cleve went into the kitchen and opened a bottle of the bourbon which he'd brought as a gift. As he filled two glasses, he called to Avant and told him to meet him on the porch. "I'll join you in a minute," Cleve said. When Cleve came to the porch, carrying the filled glasses and the bottle with the remaining whiskey, Avant had already settled himself in a rocking chair. Cleve chatted about general topics while Avant relaxed and finished his first drink. Then, as Cleve handed him a second glass of bourbon, he asked, "Have you heard about the ghost in Tom Pryor's house?"

"W-w-what do you mean?" Avant questioned, his face going white.

"Of course you know that ghosts walk this inlet," Dr. Cleve said offhandedly, playing on Avant's superstitious nature. "They always have. You mentioned it only moments ago, when you were recounting the lore of this place."

A deep flush rose from Avant's neck to his cheeks. "Yes, but that's just superstition." He drained his glass, and like a sleepwalker went to the other end of the porch and back. "They do, at that," Avant admitted. These simple words, uttered with firmness and conviction, were exactly what Cleve wanted to hear. Avant's fear was taking hold.

To Dr. Cleve, Avant looked pathetically old and vulnerable. Cleve's heart contracted with excitement as he said, "You know, my wife might be in a family way. Yours too, for all you know. If either of our wives were to see a ghost, the child of that woman would be marked for life."

Avant sighed and sat down. Cleve refilled his glass with whiskey.

"I haven't seen any ghosts in this house," Avant whispered, "but there's one next door. Alice Flagg. She died in 1849, and I've heard she roams that house and grounds."

"Everybody knows about the ghost of Alice Flagg," Dr. Cleve responded, his heart leaping. *It was working.* Avant was accepting his words as truth. "These old houses and woods are full of ghosts."

"Don't say that!" Avant cried, his face becoming twisted with worry.

Dr. Cleve watched his host intently. Avant seemed to be fighting to control himself. His eyes were clouded, and he hardly dared to breath at all.

"Don't worry about a ghost," Cleve said soothingly. "If one appears, we'll rid this inlet of him."

Avant leaned forward quickly, staring at Cleve. "We'll rid this inlet of him," he slurred in agreement.

Dr. Cleve cleared his throat. "I think we need to arm ourselves."

"Yeah. Sure." Avant hiccuped, now clearly affected by the consumption of whiskey.

Dr. Cleve excused himself for a moment and quickly left the porch and took the stairs two at a time. What was keeping Ruth? Could he get his gun without her seeing him?

He poked his head into the bedroom. Ruth, in her underclothing, was standing by a marble-topped washstand. She was sponging off as she glanced in the mirror. It was her habit to sponge off anytime she changed clothes, even if she was planning to swim. Cleve was not at all moved by her beauty as she poured water from a porcelain pitcher into a large bowl decorated with pink and yellow flowers. She squeezed a cloth and held it to the back of her neck. Her hair was pinned up in a heavy twist, but the newly grown hair at the back of her neck went into ringlets at the touch of the damp cloth. Her swimwear lay on a stool.

Cleve walked into the room. "I came to see what's taking you so long. It's getting late for a swim."

"Oh, I'll be down in a minute," Ruth answered and went back to her ablutions.

Cleve's eyes darted here and there like a snake's tongue. He opened the armoire and saw that Ruth had hung her raincoat there. Cleve's grip was also in the wardrobe. He removed his gun from it and left the room.

Back on the porch, the physician again began to talk about ghosts, and he asked Avant if Lillie Knox had ever told him any of her tales.

Avant nodded. Cleve noticed that Avant had emptied the bottle of bourbon.

Dr. Cleve eased his pistol out of a pocket and put it on the arm of his rocking chair. "See this? It's here in case we need it. Ghosts walk this land, and you can't be too careful."

Out in the inlet some fishermen splashed the water as they paddled their boats. Upstairs Ruth was wondering how cold the water would be. She went to a window. The tide was at full flood, and that was the way she liked it. And this was a star-studded night, almost artificial in its perfection. The moon was coming up and a tiny stream of light danced on the water. Ruth took her white raincoat from the armoire and slipped it on over her bathing suit.

She went downstairs barefooted and left the house by a door on the opposite side of the building from the porch, where her husband and host sat talking.

Out of a corner of his eye, Cleve could see something white moving diagonally across the grass in the darkness. He reckoned that Avant was primed enough. The time was now.

The stage was set for the drama to begin. Dr. Cleve straightened up and focused his eyes on the vision in white. "Look!"

Avant tried to focus his eyes on the wispy, white vision. Something frightening stirred within him. "Oh. Oh no. . . . It can't be . . ." he murmured.

It's working even more perfectly than I dared believe, Dr. Cleve was thinking. Avant is at this very minute frightened out of his senses. For an instant, Cleve was sad. Ruth was a lovely girl, but there was no doubt that she would blab and snitch on Smiley. All his life he'd been taught that if anything or anyone threatened the Bighams or their property, that thing or person must be disposed of without mercy.

"Shoot, man," Dr. Cleve shouted in a breathy voice, as he handed Avant the pistol. "That's a ghost!"

Avant shook his head as though to shake out cobwebs. He pointed the pistol toward the ghost and squeezed the trigger. Dr. Cleve and Avant ran to the fallen ghost. The form in white had fallen near the creek. Blood trickled downhill toward the salty brine.

"Oh, my God," Dr. Cleve cried. "You've shot my wife!"

Avant stood for a few moments, trying to grasp what had happened, then he began to cry. Some fishermen in a crudely fashioned boat heard the commotion and paddled ashore. They looked over the situation, whispered among themselves. Finally, they said that since the girl was dead, they were going for the coroner.

Neighbors who had heard the disturbance gathered on the shore. Knots of people, some crying, others shaking heads in disbelief, were huddled here and there when the coroner arrived. He began his investigation. Cleve felt hot and tired, and his shirt clung wetly to his back. He forced himself to think, to use his physician's mind. There was no way the people gathered there could possibly know his intentions; the plan had been carried out more perfectly than he had dared to dream. The coroner announced that a coroner's jury would be appointed. He would give them the results of his investigation.

"I don't know what to say," Avant mumbled as he began to sober. "I'm numb. I can't believe it."

Dr. Cleve's heart tightened when he looked into Avant's eyes, vast caverns in the paleness of a face full of pain, and he left Sunnyside, taking his and Ruth's belongings with him. He would make funeral arrangements, and after that, await the findings of the coroner's jury.

At the hearing, Dr. Cleve put up a convincing front as a bereaved husband. Ruth's family from Laurens County was there, and Cleve sensed the family wasn't convinced of his innocence. He altered his appearance to look like a grieving man. He allowed his jaw to drop open, and he held himself tensely so that his shoulder blades showed through his white shirt. He cried that his heart ached for Ruth and he longed to hold her in his arms. "What will I do without my Ruth?" That should convince them, he mused, wiping away his tears with a handkerchief. He hoped his nerve would not fail him before he had convinced the jury.

The coroner's jury decided the death of Ruth Crisp Bigham was accidental. Still, the Crisps believed there was a deception somewhere. They hadn't wanted Ruth to marry a Bigham, and they had never trusted Cleve. One of the factors supporting their suspicion was the attitude of Avant. He acted like a man who had been framed. Also, the fishermen were now saying that it was plain that Ruth was a woman and no ghost. They had recognized her as a woman as she made her way toward the creek, and they swore anyone sitting on the Sunnyside porch could plainly recognize her.

Ruth's family returned home and immediately selected Robert Cooper, solicitor of Laurens County, to represent them. He promised to go to Georgetown and convince the solicitor to reassess the case.

After studying the facts, Solicitor Wells was convinced that further legal procedure was in order. A trial date was set for Dr. Cleve and Avant. They were apprehended and locked in jail until the date of the trial. This was the first time a Bigham had ever been jailed.

Dr. Cleve was represented by Congressman J. W. Ragsdale of Florence, and Avant's lawyer was Walter Hazard of Georgetown. Congressman Ragsdale was also working on another case, one which would be tried before the Ruth Crisp Bigham murder trial. He was the defense lawyer on *The State* v. *Smiley Bigham, Daniel Hinds, and Andy Fuller*, the trial for the murder of Sam Johnson.

Back at home Smiley and Dora frequently discussed the details of Ruth's death, always marveling at the timing. How had Cleve pulled it off, they wondered? Ruth had been a woman of principles, and it had been obvious she would testify against Smiley. She needed to be stopped and Cleve had certainly seen to that.

The day of the trial in October of 1909 was hot and humid. On the front row of the visitor's section of the courtroom sat the Bighams, waving small straw fans in front of their flushed faces, which were damp with perspiration. Smiley looked back at them just before he sat down at a table before the judge's bench. Smiley, Daniel Hinds, and Andy Fuller entered a *not guilty* plea.

Although Dr. Cleve was in jail in Georgetown, he knew this was the day of Smiley's trial, and his thoughts were in that courtroom. *At least Ruth was not available to testify against Smiley.*

Sam Johnson's mother was called to the stand. She was trembling. After each question, the interrogator had to wait for her to compose herself before she could answer. Her weeping was nearly out of control, but she testified how the men had marched her son out of the house and had taken him away. She was then dismissed.

Sheriff Burch took the oath and cleared his throat. The room was stiflingly hot. He ran a hand over his forehead and slung his hand in the air; perspiration flew from it. He spoke of the boy's condition when he first saw him—clothes ripped from the body, raw bloody cuts, skin torn by thorns, the nail driven in his ear. He also mentioned that he had followed the prints of the horses' hooves to Edmund's house, but that Edmund had an alibi. The defense began its case.

Smiley's mother swore her son hadn't left the house that night. Ruth wasn't there to contradict her. Andy Flowers said under oath that he hadn't been near Smiley at the time, and Daniel Hinds said the same.

The judge charged the jury and told them that if one man was guilty, then all three were guilty. If one man was innocent, the others also were innocent. The jury left the room. They probed and analyzed, picking out a discrepancy here, an assumption there, all the while struggling to find a pattern they could accept. Finally, the verdict came from the jury. *Not guilty.* Smiley was free.

Although he was in jail, Cleve felt he'd played a strong role in getting Smiley off the hook. But he had his own trial to worry about, and he was scared.

The weather was turning cool when Dr. Cleveland Bigham and William Avant were brought to court the third week in October. It didn't look good for Cleve. With Walter Wells and Robert Cooper as prosecuting attorneys, it seemed he didn't stand a hair's breath of a chance of getting off, and as if that were not enough, Judge R. C. Watts, the state's most respected jurist, sat on the bench. But Cleve composed himself. After all, he reasoned, there wasn't a shred of evidence, nothing which could be documented, and there was no testimony which was clearly convincing or wholly acceptable.

As before, the Bighams sat on the front row. If there was a shadow of a doubt about Cleve's innocence, it wasn't evident on their faces.

Dr. Grover Cleveland Bigham was given the oath and called to the witness stand. Using medical terminology, Cleve explained the difference between mental illness and strong belief in old superstitions. Avant, he said, believed he saw a spirit. The man was on the edge of a breakdown. As Dr. Cleve was speaking, the jurors leaned forward, mesmerized, taking in every word. Some of them were very superstitious. This physician had lost a beloved wife, they believed, at the hand of a man who simply made a mistake in identity. Others wondered, how could this physician, who was saying *he* wasn't superstitious, make a mistake in identifying his own wife?

The prosecuting attorneys spoke to the court, and the jurors listened intently. Could it be possible that the educated Dr. Grover Cleveland Bigham was putting on an act? Avant was a sensible man, but he looked like a person who could be easily influenced by the powerful doctor. Had the physician brainwashed Avant? Frightened and manipulated him? And then induced him to shoot Ruth Crisp Bigham?

As the prosecuting attorneys went on with their theories, they painted a picture of Dr. Cleve taking advantage of Avant. After being cajoled and primed to kill a white ghostlike figure, when and if such a figure appeared in the darkness, could Avant have restained himself?

Avant had pulled the trigger, but Dr. Bigham was the murderer. The prosecutors rested their case.

Dr. Cleve felt a premonition of a peril closing in on him. His body was rigid, and he was cold all over. While the jury deliberated, he suddenly realized he was holding his breath, then letting it out through his mouth so there would be no sound.

After several hours, the jury returned with a verdict of guilty of manslaughter. Judge Watts sentenced Dr. Cleve and Avant to three years each in prison. Dr. Cleve's bond was posted by Dora, Smiley, and Marjorie. Avant's family signed his bond.

Immediately after the trial, the Bighams had another family conference. Dr. Cleve was assured he would never serve a day in prison. If there was one thing at which the Bighams were expert, it was outsmarting the law. This problem might take a few days to be resolved, but resolved it would be! However, there was one other matter that had to be taken care of first. One member of the Bigham family deliberately had not signed the bond, sister Leitha. Working quickly, the Bighams had five-sixths of their property deeded to Leitha and one-sixth to Marjorie. The deeds were recorded. Cleve's case would, of course, be appealed. But should the conviction of the lower court be upheld, Cleve could just disappear, and no money would be forfeited.

On April 28, 1910, Smiley went to Columbia to hear the verdict of the appeal. To his horror, the conviction of the lower court in the case was upheld. Smiley rushed back home to relay the decision to his brother. Dr. Cleve and Avant immediately left the state. But within three months Avant was recognized in Texas, apprehended, and returned to Georgetown.

Avant was incarcerated in the state penitentiary and served his three-year sentence. When he returned to Murrells Inlet he looked ill and haggard. He was never able to adjust to life with his family. Overtaken with stress, he was continually ill with inertia, an irregular heartbeat, and cold sweats. He began having hallucinations in which he fancied seeing Ruth Crisp Bigham in a white lace dress. Finally, his appetite left him, and he lost so much weight that he died of inadequate nutrition.

During the years that Dr. Cleve was moving here and there eluding the law, Edmund was living in Georgia, becoming maladjusted, sick, and prone to hysterics. Edmund was convinced Smiley would inherit the vast Bigham properties. After all, he was in Georgia and of no help to his mother, and only the Lord knew where Cleve was. Besides that, Edmund believed that Smiley was just the kind to take advantage of such a situation.

Edmund farmed a little. He planted cotton, and when it looked like he would have a good yield, his frame of mind improved. But when the boll weevil swarmed into Georgia cotton fields and left him with only a few bales, his low spirits returned. There was nothing to do but return to South Carolina and take on Smiley.

Edmund, May, Eloise, and their new little daughter, Evelyn, moved in with Smiley and Dora. But Edmund was bursting with fury as he witnessed Smiley's manipulation of his mother and supervision of the property. Also, Marjorie had converted her one-sixth share of the estate into three blank deeds, and Edmund didn't trust her motives. The suspicion that she planned to sell her share to outsiders enraged him. As time went on, Edmund was in such a constant state of rage that he was unbearable.

On January 14, 1921, Smiley rushed to the house of Mrs. Kirton, the nearest neighbor. He handed her a suitcase filled with papers and asked her to hide it. He told her Edmund had threatened to kill them all. An hour or two later, Marjorie came flying into the Kirton house, screaming that Edmund said he would wipe out the whole family. Marjorie Bigham Black, being childless, had adopted John and Lee McCracken after their mother left them. She told Mrs. Kirton she was afraid for their lives. But nothing happened that day, and everything returned to a semblance of normalcy.

But the next day was different. It was a perfect day for killing a hog, Edmund decided when he walked outside to examine the day. It was freezing cold and the sky was cloudless. Yep, it was a perfect day for a *killing*. It was Saturday, and Woodrow Wilson was president. A pound of bread cost ten cents, and a postage stamp was two cents. As the hands on the place gathered to assist in butchering the hog, Edmund hummed the favorite song of the day, "Ma, He's Making Eyes at Me," which Eddie Cantor had made popular.

By midafternoon, the hog-killing process had been completed and the farm hands dispersed. When the mailman arrived, all seemd quiet at the Bigham home. But just at that moment, Edmund, his clothing splattered with blood, ran up to the postman, who held an envelope in his hand. "Come quick!" he screamed. "The whole family has been killed."

There was no warmth in the sun which cast its rays on one of the most despicable crimes in all recorded history. Dora Bigham lay on the ground in a slime of blood. On the porch lay Marjorie's adopted boys. The three-year-old had been shot and kicked under a bench. The other boy, John, was near death, but still breathing. Upstairs, Marjorie was slumped over her sewing machine, her brains blown out. *Where was Smiley?*

To the neighbors and law officers now arriving at the house, Edmund shouted, "Smiley did it. When I got home, mama was lurching about, saying that Smiley had killed all of them. If you go across the road and into the woods, you'll likely find him dead." With everyone staring in disbelief, Edmund wandered away from the scene. He roamed around the house, and into the fields and woods beyond, until darkness fell. Finally he strolled home, like an errant fugitive. To anyone who would listen, he declared that his mother was alive when he first saw her and that she said Smiley was the murderer.

Sleep did not come to Edmund Bigham that night. He sat in a chair, a vacant look in his eyes. Before daylight someone told him that the surviving McCracken boy had passed away. Edmund bent his head to his knees and shook with a mingling of laughter and crying.

The next morning a search party set out to find Smiley. Edmund pointed out the location where he had seen his brother entering the woods just before he discovered the crime. Edmund did not join in the search. After a while he heard a yell. Smiley had been found. His remains lay in a ditch.

"All right," said the magistrate, who was one of the searchers. "Everybody form a circle around the body and hold hands. I'm going to send for the coroner, and nobody's going to disturb this evidence."

When the coroner arrived from Florence, he agreed that from all appearances, a suicide was the likely cause of death. However, he proceeded to examine the body. "The indications are, you see," he remarked, "that there wasn't no struggle involved." Half closing one eye, he examined the pockets. Smiley's wallet, which he always carried in his pocket, was missing, but Edmund's pearl-handled pistol lay in Smiley's limp hand.

Finally, the stunned people returned to the Bigham home. The coroner ordered that Edmund be searched. Edmund paused and a muscle bunched along the side of his jaw.

"It's as plain as the nose on your face that Smiley killed himself," Edmund said. But as he was searched, an overloaded wallet was found, a wallet believed to hold the contents of Smiley's missing billfold. Edmund realized the potential harm this discovery could have on his story.

Few people in the area had not heard about the murders by this time, and anyone who had an excuse came to the Bigham home to see what they could see. Although the murders had been the most heinous of crimes, people were fascinated by the actual spot where the killings had taken place. Among those who arrived was P. H. Arrowsmith, the lawyer who represented Marjorie and Smiley. He seemed to be indifferent to the events as he nonchalantly made his way about the scene. But Edmund became suspicious of Arrowsmith's snooping when the lawyer started asking the farm hands and neighbors a bunch of questions.

Burial arrangements were made. Reverend Simpson would conduct the service at ten o'clock the next morning. All five casualties—Dora, Smiley, Marjorie, and the McCracken boys— would be buried together.

Within twenty-four hours, news of the mass murder had been spread by the news services and by word of mouth. It reached every town in the state. Everyone was interested in the case from a distance and speculated on the horrible events. Some neighbors claimed they'd seen the pearl-handled pistol which had been found in Smiley's hand in Edmund's back pocket after the murders. Others believed Smiley was the queerest Bigham ever and perfectly capable of killing his own people. Someone reported that after Leitha Bigham died, her husband tried to claim the five-sixths of the Bigham estates (which were still in her name) for their son. The story was that *both* Smiley and Edmund were enraged at the idea of losing this portion to Leitha's son, or Marjorie's portion to outsiders. Someone speculated that Smiley killed his family, and Edmund merely took advantage of the situation by murdering Smiley and making it look like suicide. However, reliable details were hard to come by since the sheriff was hospitalized shortly after the murders were committed, and many people were afraid to tell what they knew.

On the day of the funeral service, people from the countryside gathered at the Beulah Baptist Church in Pamplico. Mrs. Kirton, the Bigham's neighbor, was among the mourners. As she waited for the service to begin, she noticed a strange woman walking in the cemetery. It appeared that the woman wasn't accustomed to wearing high-heeled shoes. Her ankles frequently turned and bent, and her feet were all but slipping out of the shoes. Suddenly, Mrs. Kirton's attention went to the woman's hair. It looked artificial. And other features of this strange person were also bizarre. Mrs. Kirton quietly made her way toward the stranger, and for one striking instant they locked eyes. Mrs. Kirton clearly recognized the mourner. It was Dr. Grover Cleveland Bigham.

After the services, Edmund and May and their girls went to the home of Mrs. Kirton and asked to spend the night. Mrs. Kirton was afraid for her life; she believed that Edmund was the murderer of the just-buried Bighams. But in an effort to win the confidence of Edmund and prevent him from harming her, Mrs. Kirton gave him the suitcase of papers which she had hidden for Smiley. He looked them over carefully.

"I now own all of the Bigham land," Edmund boasted to his hostess. "I'm a rich man."

A few days later, John McCracken, the father of the little boys who had been adopted by Marjorie, signed a warrant charging Edmund with the murder of his children. Before Edmund could think of an alibi he was in jail. According to the legal procedure at the time, it was decided that instead of trying Edmund for the murders of all of the victims, he would first be tried for the murder of Smiley.

On the morning of March 25, 1921, hundreds of people from Marion, Florence, and Horry counties pushed and shoved their way into the courtroom at the Florence County Courthouse to see the most celebrated, feared, and closely watched prisoner of the South Carolina prison system. Most people in the courtroom believed the case had not been "trumped up" as Edmund was claiming but that, in fact, Edmund had not only killed Smiley but had also gunned down his mother, sister, and Marjorie's adopted children. The other Bigham sister, Leitha, had died sometime prior to the murders. There were whispers and murmurings in the courtroom of others who had been wiped out by the same man. The spectators especially gossiped about the young black man who had died when Edmund drove a nail through his ear to the brain. Someone reported that when Edmund had lost eight hundred dollars to a gambler in Georgia, he killed the man, stole the money, and blamed the murder on a fellow gambler. No one was surprised by anything that Edmund Bigham had done. Like his father and grandfather, he seemed to have an inherent taste for bloodthirsty killings.

The trial was sensational, and time and time again, the judge stopped the proceedings after an uproar. No one was surprised when

Edmund was found guilty and the court pronounced punishment of death by electrocution. The judge set April 2, 1921, as the date of execution.

But Edmund was not through yet. The case was appealed to the state supreme court, and the defendant was granted another hearing for resentencing.

At the hearing on June 9, 1922, Edmund's lawyer, A. L. King, announced to the judge that he could produce a letter written by Smiley before his death, a letter in which Smiley set out his plans for killing the entire family and then himself. He said the letter had come to Edmund while he was living in Georgia. Edmund claimed he had left Georgia, at a financial loss, to go home to protect his family. Judge Shipp asked the attorney where he had obtained the letter.

"It was found by Edmund's wife, your honor." The attorney spread before the judge a letter signed *L. Smiley Bigham*, which stated that Smiley intended to kill his mother and Marjorie and then himself. King then presented affidavits swearing the handwriting was Smiley's. A frown spread over the judge's face. There were whisperings in the courtroom. Edmund sat with a sort of reckless assurance.

Solicitor Gasque was not convinced. He made the point that the handwriting of Edmund and Smiley was so similar they had previously forged one another's signature on checks. Not once, but many times. Marjorie's estranged husband, Doc Black, gave a deposition stating that the letter was a forgery. Not one phrase of that letter could have been written by Smiley, a man whose terminology and vocabulary were limited, Doc Black testified. He said Smiley Bigham had on no occasion in his entire life ever expressed himself as the letter did.

Judge Shipp's decision, which he pronounced the following day, was that the letter was a forgery. He upheld the verdict of the lower court and called for Edmund to stand for resentencing. Edmund Bigham blinked at the sudden directness. He listened intently to the words telling him that on July 10, he would die for the murder of his brother.

Edmund shouted, his voice suddenly desperate, "Judge, you remember this. I'm an innocent man. God will punish *you!*" The prisoner turned, and seeing the disbelief on the faces of those who watched him, he said nothing more. The color was gone from his face, and his bloodshot eyes were wild. Silence swept quickly through the courtroom, the sudden pressure from Edmund's outburst holding everyone speechless and still. The spectators were fascinated with Edmund, as they would have been entranced by a snake.

Soon after the courtroom had emptied, Edmund's lawyers held a conference. They agreed that if their client was ever going to receive his freedom, some shrewd, well-known lawyer would have to be called in as additional counsel. Perhaps a more expert legal mind could find an opening, if indeed there was an opening. Judge Mendel Smith of Camden was such a man. As they talked about it, the lawyers didn't believe that Judge Smith would take the case, but it was worth a try.

Judge Smith requested that the transcripts be sent to him for consideration. After studying the case, Smith accepted the challenge. He appealed for a new trial on the grounds that Judge Shipp had usurped the jury's right to decide by declaring the letter to be a forgery. And he claimed the lynch-mob atmosphere of the trial precluded a fair and impartial verdict. It was a skillful legal maneuver. Edmund Bigham was given a new trial at a hearing in March 1924. And he was given a change of venue.

On Thursday of the second week of October 1924, the Horry County Courthouse and yard were teeming with spectators.

A jury was quickly selected, and witnesses began giving testimony. Edmund's eyes locked with some of them, the eyes that exuded the I've-got-something-on-you expression. Some witnesses trembled and their voices broke in midsentence. Edmund had promised that his enemies would die "before I lie in my grave." So when one witness, George Steele, fell from the witness chair and died on the spot, many believed Edmund was responsible. The judge adjourned court until the next day.

But even that didn't compare with the drama which followed. The gruesome scene was staged by the prosecution not only to prove their case but also to unnerve Edmund.

A lawyer weaved his way through the spectators and participants in the courtroom, bearing a tray carrying Dora Bigham's skull. Some schoolchildren from the Burroughs School, who were listening to the case as a part of their course on civil government, screamed in horror.

"Mr. Bigham, this is your mother's skull. Look at it. Did you kill her?"

"No."

"Look at it!"

"No. I did not kill her."

The judge then addressed Dr. J. D. Smyser of Florence.

"Mrs. Bigham laid in the ground how long?"

"Something over three years."

"You found the body submerged in water?"

"Practically."

"You cut her head off?"

"Yes." The physician explained that when the people who had been appointed to remove a part of Mrs. Bigham's body first saw her remains, they were in fairly good shape. There were no worms or maggots about the body, but the face was not recognizable. The body was covered in mud. When the physician removed the hair of the scalp until he came to the cranium, he discovered a bullet wound on the left side at the back of the skull. He closely examined the wound at the bullet's entrance to the brain. Dr. Poston and Dr. Wilcox, he said, dished out the brains and examined them to see if there was a bullet in the skull.

The judge asked what effect such an injury would have on a person.

"The medulla being severed, you would get the same reaction as if you cut a person's head off." The physician went on to explain that any person receiving such an injury could not walk or talk.

Edmund was asked to explain his story in view of this damning testimony. Still fighting, Edmund said, "If I killed my mother may God strike me dead."

The defense team rallied, but in his closing arguments Gasque countered all the defense strategies. The solicitor spoke eloquently. Smiley's body was found, but his wallet was not in his pocket. From bloodstains on Smiley's body and a nearby tree, it was evident that the body had been moved after death. He ended his speech by pointing out that the skull theory condemned Edmund Bigham.

The jury left the courtroom. After two hours they returned with a verdict: *Guilty.* For a space of perhaps three seconds, there was nothing but silence. Then the judge's voice exploded in the room. Edmund was sentenced to die.

The case was appealed. The appeal contained some thirty-seven exceptions. A decision did not come down until early February 1926. Once again Edmund Bigham was entitled to a new trial.

Mendel Smith, Edmund's lawyer, asked for a conference with counsel for the prosecution. During the quiet time of waiting, people shifted about in their seats, whispering questions. What was happening? Would Edmund's life be spared after all he had been through, after a fortune had been spent on trials? Was a deal being made?

Finally, the court officials returned. Mendel Smith gave a powerful speech recounting the court fights for Edmund's "constitutional rights." He gave a compelling argument for Edmund as a "victim of fate." The excitement of the audience had been built up to a peak, so they felt almost cheated when Mendel Smith suddenly announced, "There will be no further testimony on either side. A decision has been reached to ask the jury to recommend mercy for Edmund Bigham. There were no witnesses to the Bigham murders."

Solicitor Gasque, who had worked on the case for six years, recommended the decision. When the jury was asked to decide on a verdict, they gave Edmund Bigham his life.

Edmund was returned to the penitentiary, but his cell was not on death row. The family who had stood by him through all of the trials now left him to his own devices. His wife May moved to Detroit with their daughters. She died there in December 1951.

In 1960, his thirty-nine-year prison term behind him, Edmund Bigham was paroled. Two years later he was dead.

As for Dr. Grover Cleveland Bigham, Edmund once confided to his lawyers that Cleve visited him in prison on several occasions. Cleve had always gone unrecognized because he was disguised as a woman.

Grandfather Leonard would have been proud because Cleve had gotten away with murder.

Will the Real Murderer Please Stand Up?

It is said that Joel Levy was the victim of one of the most diabolical frame-ups ever to be hatched in North Carolina.

On a cold and wintry day in February 1923, a man was gunned down in Cumberland County. Today, more than sixty-five years later, there are still more questions about the events of that day than there are answers.

The official record of the events started when the sheriff's department received a telephone call; someone was asking for help out at Victory Mill Lake. Deputy McLean was the first officer at the scene. When McLean stopped his car by the side of the road, B. W. Hall was sitting on a large tree stump, holding a pistol. Hall led McLean into the woods, where his friend, B. F. Strickland, was standing over a body. The fallen man was Callahan, a former Fayetteville policeman.

"What happened here?" McLean asked.

"Callahan's been shot," Hall answered.

"Who did it?" McLean asked.

"One of the two men who came in a car and hid these bags of moonshine."

"Did you get a look at them?"

"Yep."

"Know them?"

"John Smith for sure, and the other looked like that Indian, Levy."

It was bitterly cold and Callahan's condition looked serious, so McLean moved quickly. "Help me get Callahan in my car," the deputy ordered. Hall and McLean pushed the nearly comatose man into the automobile, and the two of them left for the hospital.

"Stop!" called Callahan as he regained consciousness. "The pain is too severe. I can't go on."

"But it's only a little further," the deputy answered. "It will take just a little longer."

The deputy mashed his foot on the accelerator, and the car sped ahead. He had to get the victim to the hospital fast. He asked the obvious question. "Who shot you?"

Callahan moaned, but didn't answer.

"Tell me who shot you," McLean repeated.

"I tell you I can't stand it," the injured man pleaded. "Stop the car!"

The deputy looked back at Callahan. If the man was conscious enough to beg him to stop, why wouldn't he say who shot him? "Did you see the shooting?" he asked Hall.

Hall pushed his cap back and sighed. "I was off a piece, cranking my car. I didn't see what happened. My guess would be Smith shot him."

"What do you know of him?"

"He lives at Grays Creek. A son of Madison Smith, a farmer."

"Does Smith moonshine?"

"Does he moonshine! If ever a man moonshined it's John Smith."

"We'll pick him up after we get Callahan some help." McLean turned into the hospital drive. "Did you happen to see if Callahan had a gun?" the deputy asked.

"No."

McLean eased his car over to the emergency entrance of Highsmith Hospital. Callahan was placed on a stretcher and moved into a space that was curtained on three sides. A physician and several nurses attended him. The deputy and Hall decided to wait and see what happened. At about four o'clock the physician came from Callahan's bed. He shook his head. "He's gone," the doctor said. "Too bad. The bullet apparently pierced his kidneys."

John Smith had been arrested by deputies and brought to jail when Sheriff McGeachy arrived and took over the case. Strickland and Hall were questioned at greater length about the morning's events. When asked why they were in the woods in the first place, the men said they had been "looking for fat lighter knots," pine knots rich in resin.

"When did you first see Smith and Levy?" the sheriff asked.

"We were in the underbrush when they drove up and stopped nearby," Hall answered.

"The two men emerged from the car carrying four bags, which seemed to be heavy," Strickland took up the story. "After stashing the bags in a clump of small trees, they went back to their car and drove away."

"What happened then?" Sheriff McGeachy asked.

"We walked over to the bags. They held moonshine whiskey," Hall replied.

Again, Strickland took up the tale. "Callahan—I guess in his official capacity as a special deputy and railroad cop—decided to confiscate the moonshine. He and I were standing guard over it when Smith and Levy returned."

"Who shot Callahan?"

There was a pause. "I saw Levy shoot him," Strickland finally responded.

"Hall, did you see Levy shoot Callahan?" the sheriff questioned.

"No, I only heard the shot. I was a ways off at my car."

Later that day a newspaperman hanging around the police station asked the sheriff why he was holding Smith. "Did Smith kill Callahan?"

"Smith wasn't the man who fired the shot," the sheriff answered.

"Then why are you holding him?" the reporter pursued.

The sheriff refused to comment. The reporter, if he had been given more information, might have had even more questions. Such as: Why was there such a long delay between the shooting and the time the sheriff's department received the call requesting aid? And why was Hall carrying a gun if they were just looking for lighter knots?

The following Monday, Callahan was buried in Fayetteville in a burial ground on Camden Road, between Winslow Street and Whitfield Road. On the same day, Joel Levy was arrested by deputies and placed in the Cumberland County jail without bond.

"Why has Levy been arrested?" the same newspaper reporter wanted to know.

"No comment."

"Can you tell us if he has been charged with the murder of W. C. Callahan?"

"Sorry."

"Can you tell us if John Smith is still a suspect?"

"When there is something to tell you newspaper people, we'll tell it. And we're tired of being hounded by you in regard to this case," Sheriff McGeachy remarked, staring at the reporter fixedly.

The reporter's throat tightened with anger. "Yes, sir," he replied, with sarcasm evident in his tone.

Having little information for the story, the reporter composed an article about Levy, calling him a "Croatan." At that time, there was widespread belief that the Indians living in Lumberton and Fayetteville were descendants of the Lost Colony of Roanoke.

A few days later Smith was released from custody; Levy was charged with murder. Levy's trial was set for March 10, 1923. He was represented by three lawyers, all of whom vigorously defended Levy's innocence. One of Levy's attorneys, J. Bayard Clark, was especially vocal. He stoutly maintained that the murdered man was the victim of a moonshine war—and that the man accused of killing him was a victim of the same war. He believed Levy had been framed.

But if Levy was framed, why was he framed? Was it a simple case of racism? An Indian arrested instead of a white man. Callahan had strong ties to the police department. Were they covering up something? Perhaps, in their zeal to solve the murder of "one of their own," they arrested the first person accused, without a proper inquiry. Were they covering up an incompetent investigation? Was there something more sinister involved? The questions piled up, and many people wondered if the trial would reveal what was really at the bottom of that pile.

The Levy murder trial was red-hot in the township of Pearces Mill, as well as throughout the county. Every person who could do so went to the courthouse to listen to the proceedings.

The trial began routinely. An all-male jury was to hear the case. Strickland and Hall calmly repeated the same stories they had told the police. Other witnesses corroborated their testimony. The defense called several witnesses who testified that Levy was in Fayetteville at the time of the killing. Levy denied he shot Callahan.

The theory of a moonshine war gained ground since principals in the case, as well as several witnesses, were known associates of moonshiners or had been arrested for moonshining themselves.

Then, in an unexpected move, the defense called a surprise witness to the stand. Her name was Ethel Andrews.

All three prosecutors leapt to their feet and objected to any testimony by Ethel Andrews. "Her testimony will be hearsay; it's not admissible," one shouted.

Judge J. Lloyd Horton, one of the state's youngest jurists, announced "Gentlemen, I feel that I have a higher duty than that laid down by the law. If I don't admit this testimony, I won't sleep tonight. If I admit it, I will sleep. And I don't want to stay awake. The evidence will be admitted."

Murmurs swept through the courtroom, and the judge tapped his desk with the gavel.

"Miss Andrews, where do you work?" Clark, Levy's attorney asked.

"I work at Highsmith Hospital," she answered, touching the starched collar of her nurse's uniform.

"And were you working on the afternoon of February 23, 1923?"

"Yes, sir."

"Miss Andrews, did you attend the victim, Mr. Callahan, that afternoon?"

"Yes."

"And do you recall anything Mr. Callahan said to you on his deathbed that pertains to this case?" Clark continued.

"Yes, I certainly do. He said 'The Smith man shot me.' "

"And did you tell anyone about this statement—the police, for instance?"

"The police never questioned me. But I did tell someone, Alfred de Mesquita. He asked me about the shooting victim, and I repeated what Mr. Callahan had said to me."

Alfred de Mesquita, who was the publisher of the *Fayetteville Observer*, was called to the witness chair. He corroborated the nurse's testimony and went on to say that he was a patient at the hospital when Miss Andrews spoke of the dying man.

The case went to the jury at ten o'clock that night. They discussed and argued the case until after midnight when Judge Horton ordered them locked up for the night. The next morning at ten o'clock they asked a question of the court. Back in the jury room, they continued to argue. At half past eleven they returned to the court with an announcement: they were hopelessly deadlocked.

Judge Horton ordered a mistrial. Then, in a stunning move, the judge further ordered a bench warrant for the arrest of John Smith and placed his bail at $10,000. Court was adjourned.

A few days later de Mesquita posed some serious questions in his paper. Why was Smith held but not formally charged with the slaying by the sheriff's office? Why did the judge have to do the job of the police by ordering a bench warrant for Smith's arrest? Why was no coroner's inquest held? Why were neither Callahan nor the hospital attendants questioned at the hospital by investigators? And why did the sheriff's department refuse to give out information about the killing during the first few days of their investigation?

The *Fayetteville Observer* made its disapproval of Sheriff N. H. McGeachy and his investigators crystal clear, accusing them of cloaking their inquiry with ambiguity and secrecy.

Shortly after the first trial, two events occurred which had tragic consequences for Levy. Alfred de Mesquita, who was only twenty-three, was killed in a plane crash at Pope Air Force Base. And nurse Ethel Andrews married Frank Wise of Columbia, South Carolina, and they moved to his home state.

When the new trial began, the local deputies said they had made an effort to locate the nurse, but they reported that she was "missing." Without the testimonies of Ethel Andrews and Alfred de Mesquita, the case against John Smith was weak. Smith promised the state he would testify against Levy, and the murder charge against him was dropped.

At Levy's second trial, Smith recounted the story of taking the whiskey to the woods near Victory Mill Lake. He claimed that after leaving, then returning to the scene, they spotted some men whom they believed had taken their brew. Smith colorfully described Levy pulling a pistol and firing. He maintained that he tried to prevent the Indian from killing anyone, but Levy ignored him. Smith then asserted he had never even owned a gun.

Five men were called to the stand, and each one swore that Levy was in Fayetteville on the day of the shooting. Then Charles Jones, a Fayetteville policeman, testified he saw Levy getting a haircut in a barber shop about noon on that day.

Graham Riddle swore that Hall told him that Levy wasn't the shooter; Hall had confided to him that Callahan was murdered by John Smith and John Carver.

A farmer testified that he talked with Strickland the day of the murder; Strickland told him in confidence that Smith had killed the man, not Levy.

Unfortunately, the defense was prohibited even from mentioning nurse Andrews's earlier testimony about Callahan's deathbed accusation. The stenographer's notes were missing, a rare and curious occurrence. Later it was discovered the notes had been destroyed.

The jury deliberated for two hours. They returned with a verdict of guilty. Levy received a twenty- to thirty-year prison sentence. The verdict was appealed to the North Carolina Appeals Court. The verdict of the lower court was upheld.

No one knows exactly when Levy was released from custody, but some descendants of his family said he did survive prison and upon release "went North" and never returned to Fayetteville. There are many who believe that Joel Levy was framed and that the guilty man got away with murder.

Murder in the Mansion?

Show biz. The blues. Cafe society. The Cotton Club. Rolls-Royces. Airplanes. Mansions. Dizzy dames. Dizzy house parties. Movie stars. Ziegfeld girls. Champagne cocktails. Bathtub gin. The Charleston. Skinny dipping. Murder?

"A little theme music, maestro, please . . ." "And now, ladies and gentlemen, Miss Libby Holman carries the torch of unrequited love."

A roll of drums. The tension builds.

Libby Holman, in a figure-hugging, low-cut satin gown, slinks into the island of light. In the nearly blinding light she cannot see the audience, but they can see her, and they go wild. She bows her head for a moment, then swings it up and back. The famous pout of the scarlet, Cupid's-bow lips is there for all to see. Suddenly the room is still. Libby seduces the room as she gyrates provocatively to the strains of "Body and Soul." She coaxes the audience as she moves within the circle the spotlight's radiance has created. Her dress is as brilliant as her eyes, which are flashing this way and that. Every woman in the theater wants to be like Libby, and each man wants her for his own. But only one shall have her. Although he's married, in his world of wealth and adventure, what does it matter? The romance of the stage has beckoned him.

Later, backstage, he is announced. Though he is frequently called a playboy in the press, he is stunned at the skimpiness of her attire. The queen of curves isn't disturbed that her best assets are hardly disguised by a handkerchief chemise. The Venus of Manhattan turns full circle. He stares boyishly. He is thinking that he must be at least six years her junior, but he doesn't care.

"You didn't expect me to be old-fashioned!" she says in a sultry voice, mistaking his daze for noblesse oblige.

"I think you're lovely," the heir to one of the world's great fortunes answers.

An eyebrow arches up teasingly. "I'm a star. But . . . I'm willing to be someone completely not myself in order to get the gratification of power. Can you give me power?"

"You're certainly *not* old-fashioned," he says, but he is thinking that she is a mite uppity, even if she has a right to be. Absolutely stunning, olive-skinned, throaty-voiced, New Yorky.

Leaving him to mull, she turns to another admirer. Like the tabloids say, she is wickedly entertaining. Finally, she turns back to the young man. She reaches out her gorgeous golden arm. He takes her soft hand.

And so it began.

Much later that night, he gave her a step-by-step account of his ancestry, and she was bewildered at the privileged family landscape. It was quite unlike anything she'd ever known. She learned that he came from extraordinary blood. His father was a tobacco baron. The family homes were in Winston-Salem, North Carolina. He had a brother and two sisters. He also had a wife and daughter. His life was a dynastic psychodrama of pain, rejection, and isolation created by his own unresolved torment. Although he was happiest when flying his plane, he still had dreams, and they were strong dreams.

Libby asked about the wife.

She learned that it was an evening in November 1929 when Joseph Cannon, who owned and operated the gigantic towel company, pinned down his daughter, Anne, and Zachary Smith Reynolds, teen-aged son of R. J. Reynolds, Sr., and had them chauffeured to York, South Carolina. Most people who went to York went for one purpose—to get married. Thousands of couples rushed across the state line to York, where there was no blood test or waiting period required. The hurried-up wedding uniting the South's leading financial empires was held at midnight before a groggy justice of the peace. Anne wasn't the happiest of brides, and Smith was surly. Months later, a daughter was born, and she was christened Anne Cannon Reynolds. By the spring of 1930, neither Anne nor Smith believed it would work. They even occupied separate bedrooms.

When it was Libby's turn to talk, he wanted to know everything.

Libby, born in Cincinnati, decided during college days that she wanted to be an entertainer, so she moved to New York. The decision greatly disappointed her father, a prominent Ohio lawyer. Libby, who had graduated with honors, had at one time planned to go to law school. But she had more than brains, and she wanted to conquer New York. Libby loved Harlem, went there often, and adopted the style of sultriness and gutsiness that was the fashion there. (She didn't think this was the time to dwell on Harlem because she liked this boy and hoped he hadn't heard those confounded rumors that Negro blood ran in her veins. Being from North Carolina, he would find dealing with the fact that she was a Jewess difficult enough to accept.) Now, in 1931, when most people were not working at all, and those who were made only pennies a day, Libby was commanding $2,500 a week.

"Are you a brother to the Dick Reynolds whose yellow Rolls was found in Long Island Sound?" Libby asked.

"He's not only my brother, he's a legend," Smith answered.

Libby thought it all very amusing. "What was it that he answered when questioned about the Rolls being in the sound?"

" 'I don't understand what all the fuss is about!' " They laughed uproariously. It *was* funny as Smith mimicked his brother's insouciance.

The talk got around to flying. It was his passion. His plane was his toy. She wanted to go up. On impulse they tore off to the airport. As they climbed over New Jersey, Libby was soaring with love for this romantic aviator. Flying was a new thrill for her, and she wanted to become "one of Smith's toys," and more.

And Smith Reynolds couldn't get enough of Libby either. As the days went by, he hung around theaters and watched as she made a phenomenal climb to the top of the ladder of entertainers. She became famous not only for renditions of "More Than You Know," "Moanin' Low," and "Something to Remember You By," but for "Body and Soul." "B and S," as she called it, was almost her theme song. She owed the "bluishness" of her voice to mischance. During a tonsillectomy, the knife had slipped, slitting her soft palate. Thereafter, she was known for the huskiness of her voice. Her particularly deep tonal quality and character of sound were perfect for the kind of songs she sang.

Libby had learned early to take advantage of her natural pout, throwing her head back in order for her dress to bring out the best in her. She wore her hair shoulder length and curly rather than in some of the London- and Paris-inspired cuts of the day, such as the shingle and the bob. Her dresses were based on Paris fashion, where the influence on current trends emanated from such internationally known fashion houses as Captain Edward Molyneux, Coco Chanel, and Patou. Libby, on cool nights, was often cozy in a natural gray Russian fur cape made of fine-quality squirrel skins.

With his slightly cleft chin and rather serious manner, some said Smith resembled Rudolph Valentino. But those who really got to know him learned that he could be forceful and single-minded, belying his flashy playboy image. But he did have one obsession. He believed that he might be kidnapped, and he carried a gun with him almost everywhere. Still, women found him attractive in spite of this phobia, and for a time he was even able to conceal his fear from Libby.

Their evenings usually began with Smith taking in Libby's show, always a smash due to the low-pitched, passionate vibrations of her voice. On a usual night, Libby would finish her show and wait backstage for Smith. They would leave for Tony's Westside, a speakeasy, and end up later in Harlem, usually at Jimmy Daniel's Bronze Studio or the Cotton Club.

Along with Smith and Libby, other celebrated personalities paraded through Harlem during the dark hours. Louis Armstrong, Louis Prima, Charlie Barnet, and Billy Holliday all sang there. Benny Goodman featured "Stompin' at the Savoy." Ragtime and swing had been born.

Through the fall of 1930 and into the winter of 1931 Libby had two things on her mind: young Smith Reynolds of Winston-Salem, North Carolina, and the power she generated as she walked onstage and slowly undulated into the circle of light that was the focal point of the darkened theater. She thrilled to the power of applause, and Smith was thrilled to be associated with a star. He started telling her that she should become his wife, but she didn't want to change things right at the moment. Why should they when they were running with a good crowd and going to good parties?

During the summer of 1931 both Libby and Smith took houses at Port Washington, New York. One day when Smith came to Libby's house, his eyes were glazed and Libby thought he had been drinking. He assured her he had not. As he walked around the living room, glancing here and there, he unexpectedly pulled out a gun and began waving it around. Libby screamed for him to put it away, but he promised her it wasn't loaded. He twirled the cylinder and threw it to her.

"Pull the trigger."

"No. I don't want to."

"It won't go off. It's not loaded. Pull the trigger and see."

Libby squeezed the trigger. The gun kicked and there was an explosion.

Smith laughed. "I sure thought it was empty."

Libby was scared—and furious. "*You're* empty! Empty-headed. How can you laugh when I was so frightened?"

Smith took her into his arms. "It's all right. Nothing serious happened. Just an honest mistake."

"Why do you carry a gun?" she asked.

"Libby, you don't realize how many people in my position are kidnapped for ransom. It happens all the time. I carry the gun for my own peace of mind."

She believed him. It was true. People were kidnapped for large sums of money.

It wasn't until later that summer that Libby realized Smith's fear of kidnappers was an unhealthy obsession. He spoke of *them* coming to get him, of how *they* would get him if he wasn't ready for them. On several occasions, he put a dummy in his bed as a decoy and slept under the bed, gun in hand, waiting for *them*.

The couple had fierce arguments about his behavior on occasion, but still their fascination with each other grew.

"Libby, it's time that you became my wife," Smith said one day. "Think of the life we can have together. I already have a fortune, so I'll never have to work. We can fly anywhere we choose to go."

"But you're still married to Anne."

"I can take care of that in six weeks."

Smith did just that. On October 5, 1931, he flew his wife to Nevada to establish residence in order to obtain a divorce. Six weeks later, at the final hearing, Anne was so ill and nervous that she did not attend the proceedings. She agreed to settle for a half-million trust fund for herself and another half-million trust fund for her daughter.

On November 19, 1931, Fred Schoepfer, the justice of the peace in Monroe, Michigan, married Zachary Smith Reynolds to Elizabeth Holman. A few months after the marriage, Smith convinced Libby that they would be happier at the family estate, Reynolda House, in Winston-Salem. He didn't have to do a lot of arm-twisting. She had always fancied being the mistress of a grand manor house. But until she met Smith the fantasy had seemed far-fetched. Now it was at hand.

Reynolda House was a gracious country home—airy, comfortable, and neat. It had been built in 1914 by Richard Joshua Reynolds, founder of R. J. Reynolds Tobacco Company, and his wife, Katharine Smith Reynolds. Designed by Philadelphia architect Charles Barton Keen, the house centered around the magnificent two-story living room and its cantilevered balcony. The splendid balustrade was wrought by the era's finest iron-master, Samuel Yellin of Philadelphia. The floor tiles on the porches flanking the living room were designed by the legendary Henry Chapman Mercer of Doylestown, Pennsylvania. Reynolda House marked an unprecedented development in American domestic architecture. It was designed on a magnificent scale, and yet the facial appearance was nearly as modest as that of an English cottage. Such a house was a treasure for its day.

Libby Holman, as Mrs. Zachary Smith Reynolds of Reynolda House, was well-publicized in the East. Libby loved all of it. There were snappy roadsters, snappy music, and snappy chatter. Her closets were filled with dresses embellished with frills and flounces. Even as the mistress of a famous house, Libby thought nothing of running around in her lingerie, which mostly consisted of an "all-in-one" or "step-in" garment. Visitors to the splendid mansion spoke of Libby going about "with practically nothing on." It was her way. Cafe society was in, and she was a glamour girl. After all, Barbara Hutton's coming out party at the Ritz had cost $30,000, and Barbara certainly did as *she* pleased. Libby was living a dream life in a legendary hideaway, but it wasn't long before she was beginning to miss the public.

"How can you miss Broadway?" Smith asked. "Don't you have all that anyone could ask for here?"

"Oh, darling, I do have everything and more than any girl could want. But you know . . . Broadway and Libby Holman, well they're synonymous. Perhaps you'd let me think of finding a script and only *consider* doing it?"

Smith couldn't understand Libby's love of show business. She was, in a way, a driven woman, a little hungry. In a few days Libby had convinced Smith to let her bring a drama coach to Reynolda. The coach was Miss Blanche Yurka, and Blanche brought a script with her.

Libby and Blanche spent more and more time together. Blanche was a Shakespearean actress and an excellent teacher. Libby spent most of every day speaking lines from the script to Blanche. Smith was bored with it all.

One day in June, Albert "Ab" Walker, a friend of Smith's since their boyhood, stopped by to chat with the young Reynoldses. They invited him to stay for dinner. Conversation was lively, and both Libby and Smith enjoyed the camaraderie. Walker was not employed, so Smith made him the offer of a job.

"What sort of work?" Walker asked.

"You can be my secretary," Smith answered.

"Your secretary, for heaven's sake? What do you need a secretary for?"

"I need one. And I also need an assistant on my long-distance flights. Will you take the job?"

"I'll take it," Walker said. He and Smith shook hands.

Walker went to his parents' home on Country Club Road, a fashionable section of the city. He told them that he was moving into Reynolda House and would work as Smith's secretary. Later that night he moved into a guest bedroom on the second floor of the mansion. The room had once been Smith's room, but now Smith and Libby occupied the glassed-in sleeping porch at the end of the hall. On the second floor of Reynolda, there now lived Libby and Smith, Ab Walker, and Blanche Yurka. They were like a family, and Libby continued to sashay around in the filmiest and skimpiest of lingerie.

During that month Libby's family came from Cincinnati for a visit. Libby joyfully escorted her mother, father, and sister about the gracious estate, showing them the house, its wide porches, cultivated gardens, and Lake Katharine, which was surrounded by woodland. Smith, usually with a highball in a hand, stayed to himself as much as possible in order to avoid long conversations about Libby's ancestors. Although Libby had indulged her parents by listening to the family stories, they held no interest for Smith. But on one occasion, he perked up his ears and listened.

The story was about Libby's father's grandparents, who had come from Germany in the mid-1800s. But Libby's mother interrupted the tale to tell about her five sisters and her parents, David and Elizabeth Workum, who had gone to Cincinnati from New Orleans in 1829. And then the story went back to a former generation, when Benjamin Cohen married Rachael Shenon. Smith stormed from the room. From what he had heard, he concluded that surely Libby was a Jewess.

Libby made no apologies for Smith's behavior. She just whispered to her parents that he had heard rumors referring to her as "the Yankee Jewess" who had taken over Reynolda House. Her father was embarrassed and angered over the gossip. What was wrong with being Jewish? In Cincinnati he was an outstanding lawyer and citizen. He had provided well for his family, and Libby had been brought up in a rather special lifestyle. Their maid, Mattie, had spoiled her and carefully supervised her diet, dress, and manners.

But Libby knew that Smith, in conservative Winston-Salem, would have second thoughts about a Jewish wife. Even if he could resign himself to being married to a Jewess, what would the Winston-Salem grapevine do with the news? They would grab it like a starving dog grabs a bone.

Tension began to build between Libby and Smith. Libby spent more time than usual with Blanche Yurka, and Smith scrutinized Libby through narrowed eyes as she spoke her lines. It wasn't the best of times for Smith in another respect. His kidnapping phobia had been heightened by the snatching of ten-month-old Charles Augustus Lindbergh, Jr. A ransom demand had been found some hours after the child's disappearance. Subsequent notes were received. Mrs. Lindbergh, who was expecting another baby, was frantic. Smith pictured the cold wind on the night of March 1 banging shutters and rattling windows of the house on the New Jersey estate, a place much like Reynolda. Smith checked his gun, which he kept on the porch where he and Libby slept.

Finally, Libby had all she could take of Smith's moods. She tried to think of something to reduce the strain Smith was under. She hadn't ever known him to be so high-strung and nervous.

"What do you say we have a party?" Libby asked one day.

"A big blowout?" Smith questioned.

"Oh, no. Nothing elaborate. Just a few of our Winston-Salem friends. We haven't had a party, and I think it would be fun."

"It would be nice to get a group of friends together. How does the idea of a barbecue by the lake sound to you?"

"Oh, Smith, that would be perfect."

"You're sure you don't have in mind bringing some celebrities down from New York?"

"Absolutely not. I don't want any 'sparklies' at this party."

"Then go ahead. Make the preparations."

"I'll work on the list and we'll talk it over."

It was working! Smith was relaxing and seemed more like himself. But Libby still couldn't get her mind off the script that Blanche Yurka had brought. The very idea of a play thrilled Libby and filled her with anticipation. At night, while Smith slept, she stared into the darkness as she pictured her entrance on the New York stage, her exit, the audience, the reviews.

The next Sunday as Smith and Libby talked about their party, Blanche walked in the room. She had the script under her arm. Libby turned from Smith and told Blanche she was ready to rehearse. Smith was infuriated.

"I'm getting away from this," he barked to Ab Walker.

"Where do you intend on going?" Walker asked.

"I don't know. But let's go."

Smith and Walker checked into the Robert E. Lee Hotel and proceeded to get very tipsy.

"I do believe the illustrious Mr. Reynolds is under the influence," Walker jibed.

"And his secretary, Mr. Walker, is three sheets to the wind," Smith wisecracked.

The next morning they checked out and went back to Reynolda House.

"Oh, Smith," Libby said when he arrived home. "I've decided that the party will be in celebration of Charlie Hill's birthday."

That was fine with Smith. Charlie Hill was a good friend, and a fellow aviator. He was one man with whom Smith had something in common. But for the life of him, Smith couldn't conceive of why Libby wasn't angry that he had spent the night in a hotel. Didn't she care anything about him, he wondered?

"And in addition to Charlie, we'll invite some others." Libby went on to name Babe Vaught; Jim Shepherd, an art shop proprietor; Charlie Norfleet, head of the trust department of Wachovia Bank and Trust Company; and Lewin McGinnis, operator of the airport. "And of course I'll come up with some other names."

"Sounds like a motley bunch," Smith answered, still wondering why Libby wasn't annoyed he had spent the night away from home.

As Libby and Smith continued with plans for the party, Libby brought up the idea of getting a New York apartment. Smith wasn't crazy about the idea. "It's Blanche's doing. She's turned you around, and all you can think of is New York and the stage."

"Blanche has nothing to do with it. Nothing at all. It's *my* idea. We can afford it, and we enjoy New York. If there is any reason why we can't have our own apartment there, then I'd like to hear it. We'll announce it at the party. That bunch will drop dead when they hear what we're planning."

The day of the party, July 5, finally arrived. Libby, in a flimsy chemise and high heels, held a drink as she eyed the outfits in her closet. The side of the long room that was allocated for dresses was jam-packed with flashy gowns. Libby took one and then another, holding them in the light, but none suited her. Finally she decided on white satin hostess pajamas, trimmed in lace. She loved to wear white because it showed off her dark skin.

Libby allowed herself time to linger in a tub of water heavy with the scent of lilacs. She loved cologne and used it lavishly, especially in bath water. Now and then she reached for a glass and took a sip of bourbon as she mused on the evening that stretched ahead.

After the bath, Libby wiggled into a chemise and the hostess pajamas. She brushed her hair, dabbed a slash of red on her lips, and splashed a handful of cologne on her hair and neck. Glancing in a mirror, she was all but mesmerized by her own beauty, grace, and sophisticated stylishness. Not permitting herself to tarry long before the mirror, she flew downstairs and joined Smith and Walker on the porch. Blanche Yurka walked up and was offered a highball but turned it down. She said she planned to stay in her room and not join the party. Libby grabbed the drink offered to Blanche and downed it.

"You're going to be pie-eyed drunk before the guests arrive," Smith admonished his wife.

"So what's it to you, Bub?"

Packards and other big cars, including a Rolls-Royce and an English Daimier limousine, pulled into the circular driveway. As the guests came in, they were jolly and frolicsome. It was plain to see that they were eager to party with the young Reynoldses. As they gathered on the porch, Smith ambled over to his wife. "You're drinking too much. Slow down." He was furious. She was a Yankee, a Jewess, and a drunk, and for all he knew she probably *did* have Negro blood in her veins. He was suddenly embarrassed for his Winston-Salem friends to talk with her. Almost any young lady in Winston-Salem would have made a better showing as the mistress of Reynolda than Libby was doing. She wasn't the kind to appreciate such an estate.

Libby turned on a radio and moved the dial from station to station. When she picked up music from the Grill Room of the Hotel Pennsylvania, she began to dance the Charleston.

"Pile it on, girl," someone said.

Smith went to the radio and turned it off.

Just then Blanche Yurka unexpectedly joined the group. When she suggested a canoe ride, they all left the porch for the lake. More drinks were served as the party-goers moved to the barbecue pit, but Smith wasn't drinking much. He seemed more interested in the drink that Libby was accepting.

"Canoe ride anyone?" someone called out.

"Not for us," Smith answered for himself and Libby. She was in no shape to climb into a boat.

A young man helped Blanche into a small boat and jumped in just as he pushed it onto the water. As the tiny vessel floated away from the shore, some members of the party were joking boisterously. Libby was laughing almost hysterically. Blanche was the only one who had not had a drink. After a while the canoe came back to shore, and Blanche excused herself. Although some barbecued ribs were offered, she refused and started back up the hill toward the house.

For a while, everyone munched on the ribs and chatted in a friendly manner. Libby hadn't let up in her drinking, and she soon went over to Babe Vaught and suggested that they compete in a drinking contest.

"Oh, let's," the young woman answered.

Libby took two glasses and began to sip from both.

"How 'bout a little torch song, Libby?" someone asked.

Smith was ill at ease. What was Libby up to?

"Yeah," Walker called out. "Libby give us a little uh, one, uh, two."

That Ab Walker, Smith thought self-consciously, is going along with Libby. He's egging her on. What's wrong with him?

Someone helped Libby climb up on a picnic table. Her luminous eyes sparkled. She held her head back and her face went into the famous pout. There was laughter. "Way to go, Libby," Walker shouted.

Everyone other than Smith seemed relaxed and friendly. He had watched Libby all night and her behavior had astounded him. She was flirting outrageously with Ab Walker, who appeared to be fascinated. And Walker looked so juvenile in that white bathing suit with a red cross on it, Smith thought. He looked like a Boy Scout!

Libby swayed back and forth, her mouth slightly agape, as she stood on the table. "No songs tonight, boys," she slurred.

"Ab, you're acting like a stage-struck schoolboy," Smith scolded. "Get hold of yourself."

Walker shrugged a shoulder. What was wrong with Smith? He was a self-conscious wallflower, but that didn't have anything to do with

Libby. Smith was younger than Libby, much younger, but he was already an old man! Libby's tinkling laughter at a risqué remark drifted
over to them. "Push on," Walker warned Smith distractedly. "Shove
off!"

The merrymaking was reaching its peak now, and Libby, still on the
table, was bending over, her provocatively low-cut pajamas intimating
just how daring she really was. She smiled warmly at Walker, and he
inclined his head toward her. Her movements were suggestive and her
voice sultry as she went into the lyrics of "Body and Soul." Her voice
was so low it was almost a moan.

Finally, the party started to wind down. The contest with Babe
Vaught had blurred into oblivion. The party began to break up, and
one by one, the guests said their good-byes to Smith.

"Good night, Smith. Had a good time."

"Thanks for coming," Smith answered.

"Hey, Smith, you can give a good one."

"Thanks. Any time."

"Night, Smith."

"Take care, buddy."

Smith walked back up to the house and out to the driveway, where
he helped his guests into their cars. When he went back down to the
lake, he looked around for Libby. She was nowhere to be seen. He heard
someone plunge into the lake. Then another. Giggles came from the
water.

Smith trudged back toward the mansion. Libby had started drinking
too early and she had kept it up, he thought. And that slob Ab Walker
was no better. What was he going to do about them? He sat down and
looked out into the darkness. Somewhere a dog barked.

Under his steady gaze, Smith saw Libby stumbling up the hill toward
the house. Smith went down to her and took her by the arm. Vivid
grass stains smudged her satin pajamas. "I'm going to bed," Libby said.

Just then Walker showed up. He still has on that revolting bathing
suit, Smith thought somewhat distractedly. Walker followed Libby and
Smith into the house.

Sometime later Blanche Yurka awakened with a start. Someone was
downstairs, talking. Blanche had napped during the party, since she
thought that at forty-five she was too old to be kicking up her heels
with the young crowd. She looked at her watch. Hmmmm. Nearly one
o'clock. She pulled on a silk dressing gown and went to the balcony and
looked down on the living room. No one was in sight. She made her

way down the stairway. When she saw Walker locking up for the night, she went back upstairs to bed. Sometime later, she awoke to the sounds of hysteria. Was it mirth or fear or illness? Blanche couldn't be sure. She pulled on her dressing gown and again ran to the balcony. Leaning over, she saw Walker downstairs. The silly boy was still in his bathing suit. And just then an agonizing cry split the air. Walker ran upstairs. Blanche recoiled against the wall. Walker ran to the sleeping porch, and in a moment he and Libby came out, both bending over something. They were pulling Smith's body, which was dead weight.

"Help me get Smith to the hospital," Walker requested.

"What happened?" Blanche cried.

"He shot himself."

"Oh, dear Lord, no."

Libby was screaming. She seemed overwrought with fear. Somehow they got Smith's body in the car and made their way to Baptist Hospital. Walker still had on his white bathing suit, and Libby was clad only in a dressing gown that kept gaping open and revealing her naked body. She didn't notice it or didn't care.

At 5:25 a.m., Smith Reynolds was pronounced dead. The coroner announced that the death was a suicide.

However, because Ab Walker gave contradictory statements, the sheriff later went to Reynolda House to question him. First, Walker had said that he found Smith stretched out on top of Libby. Later, he had stated that when he first saw Libby, she was running down the hall.

As Sheriff Scott sat in Walker's room taking notes, he noticed a pair of women's shoes under the bed.

"Look at those," he said.

"Yes," answered Walker.

"Whose are they?"

"Libby's."

"Why are they here in your room?"

"I don't know. She must have come in here with Smith."

After they had talked a while, the sheriff got right to the point.

"Why do you think she did it?"

Walker put his head in his hands. "Dammit, that's something I'll take to my grave."

Reporters from all the big eastern newspapers were sent to Winston-Salem. By the time they arrived on the scene, the big house was closed to them. They flew about the town, trying to get any scrap of information about the death. But law enforcement officers remained quiet, only admitting that they were trying to clear up certain matters. Some-one asked if Libby would inherit Smith's large inheritance.

"I can't say," an official stated. "It may go to the courts." On further investigation, it was revealed that the will of the late R. J. Reynolds provided that any of his children could appoint an executor for his es-tate by will. (But Smith had not yet come of age. As a minor, Smith could not make a legal will. If he had made a will, he would not have been assigning or transmitting to his heirs any of his personal property, but willing his share of an estate.)

The question of Smith's first wife was raised. However, the former Mrs. Reynolds had waived all claims for herself and her child in accept-ing a million-dollar settlement at the time of her divorce in Reno.

At the time of his death, Smith Reynolds was twenty, and Libby was either twenty-six or twenty-eight, depending on which record one chose to believe. Smith was given a simple funeral. Libby's family had arrived, as had Smith's. The family sat quietly in the reception hall of Reynolda House as the minister conducted the rites. Libby, dressed in mourning, sat between her mother and father. Now and then she wept. Her mother comforted her. The family then followed the corpse to Winston-Salem Cemetery, where Smith was laid to rest beside his father in the family plot.

Court officials had made a decision to keep the matter of an inquest secret until after the funeral. Coroner W. N. Dalton, who had previ-ously recorded a verdict of suicide, met with the solicitor, Carlisle Hig-gins, and the sheriff, Transou Scott. In spite of the original suicide verdict, the sheriff insisted upon continuing the investigation.

Thirty minutes after the burial, a coroner's jury met in the library at Reynolda. Among the subjects that were discussed were the bullet wound, the skin that was slightly powder-burned, and the belief that Libby and Walker were inebriated. Libby testified that she remembered nothing for a forty-hour period beginning the morning of the party, ex-cept for one instant when she heard Smith call her name followed by a burst of light. She appeared to be near collapse and was sedated with opiates.

Walker remembered going to the sleeping porch and finding Smith lying across the bed, his face in a pool of blood. There had been blood in Libby's bathroom, and smears on the door facing. The body was then pulled down the long hall to the divided stairs, and down to the drawing room. But Ab had no explanation for the fact that no blood-stains were found on this path, while there was a bloodstain under his bed. As to the gun, Walker said he couldn't figure out what had happened. The first time the police looked for it in the death room, it wasn't there. Later the gun mysteriously appeared on the floor of the sleeping porch.

As the days passed, more information filtered into the office of the sheriff. Smith Reynolds was left-handed, but the bullet entered the right side of the head. The sheriff formed an opinion that Smith did not shoot himself. Another grand jury met in the Forsyth County Courthouse. *Libby and Ab Walker were charged with the murder of Smith Reynolds.*

At midnight on August 23, the body of Smith was exhumed from its grave for a secret autopsy. Four of the city's most renowned surgeons were on hand for the examination of the head wound. In order to fully explore the entrance contusion, the scalp was peeled back. The physicians scanned the passageway of the bullet. They also inspected the exit passage behind the left ear. Then, quietly, the body was settled back in the coffin, much in the manner a new mother might tuck her baby in its cradle. Before dawn, all was as it had been at the cemetery.

The curiosity of the whole nation was now piqued by the case. Libby had announced she was pregnant, and the news of Smith's child gave the case even more drama. But the highest drama of all was centered around the trial.

On the afternoon of October 14, Carlisle Higgins let it be known that he would hold a news conference. Reporters thronged into his office, expecting to learn the date of the trial.

"I want you to know that I will consider two alternatives," he explained. "I can ask for a nol. pros. with leave." A nolle prosequi (nol. pros.) meant that he could return the defendants to their status before they had been indicted for murder. However, under this procedure, he also had the option of restoring the case to the court docket at any time simply by obtaining from the grand jury a report of the indictment.

"On the other hand, I can ask for continuance, which means a postponement of the case."

The hearing was to come up the next day, and everyone was frantic to know which choice the solicitor would make. There were mild speculations, as well as serious wagers of money. Finally, the next day came, and the people took their seats in the courtroom. They whispered, still wondering what would happen. Higgins was a hard man in court, that much everyone knew.

The door opened. There was a hush. Higgins came in quickly and sat down. "I have decided on my course."

Practically all of the evidence in the case had been presented to the coroner's jury, Higgins pointed out. That evidence had been carefully considered. Additionally, all of the witnesses who had attended the party had been questioned by that jury. Considering everything that had been examined, and all of the statements that had been made, the solicitor said that he was requesting a nol. pros. be entered in the case.

Ab Walker and Libby were free. The reporters looked at each other quizzically. There were so many unanswered questions in the case. Were the authorities trying to build a stronger case against Libby and Ab, or did they believe there just wasn't enough evidence for a conviction? Or did Smith Reynolds really commit suicide? After all, he *was* highstrung, and he was known to experience periods of depression and anxiety, when his fear of kidnappers was greatest. Maybe Libby's innocent—or not so innocent—flirtation with Ab drove Smith over the edge. But why was that bloodstain under Ab's bed, and where was Walker's gun? Smith's gun mysteriously showed up on the sleeping porch, but Ab's was never found.

Most of the questions remained unanswered. But Libby and Ab Walker were never charged again with the murder, and on January 10, 1933, at 6:48 p.m., a son was born to Libby Holman Reynolds. He was named Christopher. The question on everybody's mind was how much of the twenty million dollars, believed to be Smith Reynolds's portion of his father's estate, would belong to Libby's child. A law firm announced that they had been retained to represent Libby and her son. However, Libby's father let it be known that Libby would be agreeable to a compromise.

Meanwhile, Anne Cannon Reynolds, Smith's first wife, was reading the papers, and it dawned on her that she had settled for a paltry sum. She wanted to get into this ball game, too.

In the autumn of 1935, after much public haggling, Heriot Clarkson, associate justice of the North Carolina Supreme Court, wrote a decision that ended forever the scramble for Smith's inheritance. A foundation in the name of Zachary Smith Reynolds was created, which would over the years award grants to charitable causes. (Libby's father had come up with this idea.) Settlements from Smith's estate included $50,000 to Albert Walker; $500,000 to Libby Holman Reynolds; $500,000 to Anne Cannon Reynolds; $2,050,000 to Anne Cannon Reynolds II; $2,000,000 to Christopher Reynolds; and $7,210,900 to the Smith Reynolds Foundation. (Smith's brother and two sisters added funds from their personal money in order to substantially build the foundation.)

In a few years Libby was back with the Broadway crowd, but the whirligig wasn't as fast and crazy as it had been in the old days. She starred with Ilka Chase in an operetta, *Revenge with Music*, which ran for 158 performances. The following year, Jean Harlow played Libby in a movie based on the Smith Reynolds death. Libby still had stardust in her eyes, and she still played the nightclub and cabaret circuit. But most of all she seemed to play the part of a wealthy aristocrat. After all these years, she had come to love respectability. In 1939 she married Ralph de Riemer Holmes, an actor. Again, Libby had married a younger man. But a war was coming and he was going away to serve with the Army Air Corps.

Libby acquired a luxurious country home in Connecticut, which she named Treetops. Once again she settled down to become mistress of the manor. When the war was over, her husband returned, but he didn't go to Libby's Connecticut home. Instead, he made his home in a New York apartment. It was there that Captain Holmes was found dead at the age of thirty, a victim of an overdose of sleeping pills.

By 1948, Christopher was in his teens, and Libby made another attempt at show business. She was older now, and her appearances didn't bring the adulation she had expected. Again, she went home to Treetops. In August 1950 she was in Europe when seventeen- year-old Christopher left for a mountain climbing trip with a friend from New York. The boys arrived at Mount Whitney in California early on a Sunday morning. When they left for the climb, they assured a park employee they had climbed the Alps and were excellent climbers. Several days later, their bodies were discovered. Christopher was crumpled in a crevasse about two hundred feet from the peak.

Treetops was the sanctuary Libby needed. The rooms were large and filled with fresh flowers from the greenhouse. She greeted all who called on her, and a collection of cake plates was put to good use. Libby served beautifully decorated cakes on exquisite crystal plates. The dessert was usually accompanied by café noir. But Libby was to find out that even Treetops didn't bring her the peaceful seclusion she desired after the death of her son. She went to Europe, where she was surrounded by international celebrities. She finally returned home and found great peace of mind with an old friend, Jennings Perry. One night while they were together she made a pronouncement that was a match in sensationalism to Ab Walker's famous statement: "Dammit, that's something I'll take to my grave."

That night Libby must have desired self-purification, or perhaps self-punishment. At any rate, Perry was leaving on a writing assignment when she suddenly asked, "Jennings, how would you like to make a million dollars?" She went on to say that she was willing to tell him exactly what had happened at Reynolda House, and he could write it. Unfortunately, the overture didn't come at an appropriate time for Jennings. He turned down the offer, or at least didn't get back to it when he returned.

In her last years, Libby lived with her third husband, Louis Schanker, on her elaborate 112-acre estate in Connecticut. Occasionally they went to Manhattan and took in some shows, and on those occasions they stayed at Libby's apartment. It was a quiet time, a good time, but Libby desired to own still another extraordinary house. She found such a dwelling at East Hampton, on Long Island.

In June 1971, Libby Holman Reynolds Holmes Schanker died at age sixty-two. She was dead when her body arrived at a Stamford, Connecticut hospital. A month later, Libby's death was ruled a suicide.

There were three people who knew what really happened that night at Reynolda House. Ab Walker said he would take the knowledge to his grave, and obviously he did. Libby offered to tell the story to Jennings Perry, but he didn't get around to it in time. When Blanche Yurka, the only person who wasn't drinking on that fateful night, was questioned toward the end of her life, she agreed to tell her story for a sum of money. However, her offer wasn't accepted. She has since died.

And so, the whole story of Zachary Smith Reynolds's death on July 6, 1932, was never told. The circumstances of the death are still a mystery.

Murder on Meeting Street

On November 1, 1933, a baffling murder took place in Charleston. It involved one of the city's most prominent women. The circumstances were so strange that for years there wasn't even general agreement that it *was* a murder.

Why don't you decide?

On that fateful November evening, Mrs. John Ravenel was returning to her home on Tradd Street from a dinner with friends at the Fort Sumter Hotel. Mary Ravenel, like other Charlestonians, enjoyed "genteel entertainment," which usually consisted of an elegantly served meal followed by spicy conversation. And no one could spice their conversation quite so flavorfully as Mrs. Ravenel.

Many years before, while a young woman, Miss Mary Mack of Detroit had married William Martin, the owner of several plantations in the vicinity of Savannah. William Martin died in 1903, leaving Mary with four children to raise. But her second marriage three years later was more fortunate. She married a man of "the quality"—John Ravenel, a son of St. Julien Ravenel. St. Julien had studied medicine in Philadelphia and France. He had a large plantation called Stony Landing and a substantial medical practice, and he had developed the first limestone mining works in the state on his plantation. His son John was a prominent businessman. Mary's origins were of scant social importance once she had married into the Ravenel family.

Mary especially loved the mansion on East Battery; even women in magnificent clothing and jewels from Paris had their drivers slow their automobiles in order to get a better glimpse of the house. The twenty-four rooms, five halls, six baths, four stairways, and seven black-marble mantels were spectacular. Walls were thirty-two inches thick, and recessed paneling and a high chair rail decorated the second-floor drawing room, which permitted a grand view of the harbor.

It was a good marriage for Mary, although John preceded her in death by many years. After his death, she moved to the house on Tradd Street, where she entertained often. No doubt Mary had her good qualities. She was active in her church and in the community, and she was said to be loyal and devoted to her friends. But she also had a wicked tongue, often employed in gossip.

One of Mary's favorite topics of conversation was "that effeminate man, the photographer," who lived at the corner of Meeting Street and Price's Alley. So frequently had he been maligned by Mrs. Ravenel as she gorged herself with Low Country foods that word of the idle rumors got back to the photographer, Mr. Payne. But, it didn't slow down the tittle-tattle of Mrs. Ravenel. After dinner, or over a bridge table, she buzzed the latest scandal of the port city.

Since Mrs. Ravenel lived in the historic section of Charleston where the blue bloods lived, she was part of the highest social stratum of the city. Although some members of the plutocracy were becoming bored with her chatter, she nevertheless was received in all the most fashionable circles. Evidently she was never dashed by any criticism; there were many people in Charleston who savored every tidbit of her gossip.

The evening of November 1 was balmy as the celebrated resident strolled past the stately old homes on Meeting Street. It was her wont to amble amidst the oaks, huge magnolias, and white-columned houses as she went back and forth to her usual haunts, mainly the Fort Sumter Hotel on the Battery. On this evening, she had not a worry in the world. Some cats yowled as she approached Water Street. The chimes of a church bell struck the quarter-hour. Just at that moment, a man loomed before her. She screamed and raised her right arm to ward off an attack. It was over in an instant. Her attacker took off, and as he ran, he looked back over his shoulder at Mrs. Ravenel. She screamed a second time just before she slumped to the ground.

Some minutes later, as Elsa Eberhard drove by the corner of Water and Meeting streets, she saw what appeared to be a body lying on the sidewalk. Pulse racing, Elsa drove as fast as she could to a nearby fruit store, where she asked Johnny Townsend, who was a sophomore at the College of Charleston, for help. He got into her car, and they sped to the scene.

Johnny jumped out of the car and turned the body over. "Oh my word," he blurted. "It's Mrs. Ravenel." The thought occurred to Elsa that not only did most of the residents in Charleston know Mrs. Ravenel, but the students at the college recognized her as well. Mary's purse was by her side. It was undisturbed, and her expensive jewelry was intact. As Mrs. Ravenel began to moan and babble incoherently, they could see that she was injured. They quickly got her into the car and took her to Roper Hospital.

Mary was still conscious when they arrived at the hospital, and when a nurse asked the patient the name of her physician, she was able to give her the name. A call was placed to his home.

"What happened to you?" an attendant asked the patient as they awaited the arrival of her doctor.

"A man hit me."

"Was he driving an automobile?" Because she was able to speak and there was no visible wound or bleeding, the hospital staff evidently guessed she had been struck by a car.

"I don't know," Mrs. Ravenel answered weakly.

The nurse returned to say that the physician could not be located. Did she have another one in mind? Since the patient didn't appear to be severely injured, hospital workers took their time to see that she was treated by a doctor of her choice. She gave them the name of two others. But before they arrived, Mary Ravenel died.

A hospital doctor quickly examined the body and concluded that Mrs. Ravenel had been stabbed. Before a more thorough examination could be made, a car from the funeral home arrived, and the body was taken away to prepare for burial. But within a few minutes after the body arrived at the mortician's establishment, a wound was discovered in Mrs. Ravenel's arm. She had been shot.

Dr. Kenneth Lynch, professor of pathology at the Medical College of South Carolina, was summoned to perform an autopsy. During the inspection of the body to determine the cause of death, it was found that the bullet went cleanly through the forearm and pierced Mrs. Ravenel's heart. The bullet was of the .38-caliber copper-jacketed type, which was not common. There was evidence that it had been hand-filled. No powder burns were found, and it could not be determined from what distance the shot was fired. There was almost no external bleeding; Mrs. Ravenel had died of internal hemorrhaging. The body was bruised, and it was surmised that Mrs. Ravenel had dragged her body a few feet before collapsing.

By this time police had arrived at the scene of the crime. A crowd had gathered, and residents of that area were questioned. Someone had heard a gunshot at a quarter to ten. Another person had heard a cat crying loudly. Someone else had heard a woman scream and a car drive away. Others had heard the steps of a man or woman running. Someone said that Mrs. Ravenel had screamed twice. As the officers summed up the evidence, they really had little to go on; there was no weapon at the scene—and no eyewitnesses.

At eleven o'clock on November 3, 1933, as funeral services for Mary Ravenel were being held at her home at 12 Tradd Street, police were no closer to discovering what had happened.

The days passed, and as the authorities continued their investigation into the murder, more than forty theories were formulated. Some people believed that the killer was shooting at cats, and accidentally hit the woman. But why didn't that person step forward and admit it if the shooting was an accident? Others believed robbery was the motive. They said the robbery scenario was supported by the testimony of neighbors who claimed they heard a scream both before and after the pistol shot. The first scream would indicate Mrs. Ravenel was frightened. After all, she wouldn't have screamed before the shot if she had been hit by a stray bullet meant for a cat. But why weren't her jewelry and money taken? Most of those who voiced an opinion did not think that Mrs. Ravenel was murdered deliberately. She was a pillar in the community, and it was unthinkable to them that she would be gunned down on purpose.

If the death was intentional, then it seemed to have been a perfect crime. No one saw it. No gun was found. No motive could be ascertained. The wound was even such a clean shot that it wasn't discovered until some time after the fact.

Still, the investigation continued. On November 27, Robert Cox, a nineteen-year-old Charleston man, was questioned. He lived at 42 Vanderhorst Street, which was not in the immediate vicinity of the crime. However, he had confessed to participation in two nearby store holdups. But Cox staunchly denied any connection with the killing of

Mrs. Ravenel. No evidence to the contrary was ever found, and Cox was not charged in connection with the death.

Mayor Burnet Maybank, in an effort to urge anyone who had a clue to come forward, offered a reward of $250 for "information leading to the apprehension and conviction of the person or persons responsible for the death." He added, "There are no strings attached." Anyone who had even a scrap of evidence was urged to bring it in immediately. But the reward went unclaimed.

Three years passed, and during that time many pistols were examined, but none was the murder weapon. The use of ballistics in identifying weapons by the marks they made on bullets fired from them was not commonly practiced in Charleston at that time, but it was known that the .38-caliber pistol that was used in the killing of Mary Ravenel had fired a copper-jacketed, hand-filled bullet.

Finally, police thought they had a lead. On April 2, 1938, William Allen was found dead in Blackstone, Virginia, with a shotgun at his side. In a suicide note found on the body, he confessed to the murder of a local woman and wrote that he also had killed a woman in Charleston. The Ravenel case was the only unsolved murder case in Charleston at that time.

The Ravenel case was reopened. The chief of police detectives Joseph Wise, left Charleston for Blackstone in an effort to solve the mystery. He was accompanied by Detective James Atteberry. However, after a full investigation, the officers conceded that Allen was not the murderer of Mrs. Ravenel. Furthermore, they believed that Allen had called attention to Charleston only because a divorced wife lived there at the time the note was written. The portion about Charleston was apparently written to embarrass his former wife.

Just when it seemed the perfect crime really had been committed, nature took a hand in the unraveling of events. At least some people believe so.

It was a Wednesday night, and all was calm on the peninsula of magnificent and historic homes. As the people of Charleston lay snug in their high-poster beds on the night of September 28, 1938, they were unaware that a small tropical disturbance had formed in the eastern Gulf of Mexico.

By Thursday morning, low-hanging clouds, pushed by strong upper winds, covered the city. As her children got ready for school, and her husband drove into the city, one woman stood on the widow's walk of her house, her eyes searching the sky over James Island. It was an ominous sight. A huge, black funnel cloud that had only minutes before touched down at Edisto Island, twisting huge trees and exploding houses, was now dropping onto James Island. The woman rushed back downstairs to gather her children in the middle of the house.

At about eight o'clock, some men standing at the front of a filling station saw the black spout approaching from the west bank of the Ashley River. As it increased in velocity, it sucked up water from the river it was crossing. As the tornado reached the river bridge, it lifted a huge truck, spun it around, and dumped the shattered wreck on the ground. The men at the filling station were horrified as they watched the massive cloud come closer. In an instant the roof of the gas station where they were standing flew off and splintered.

Robert Aldridge, the meteorologist at the weather bureau, was making a call about the storm when he spotted a second funnel, following almost precisely the same path as the first. "My God, a second one is coming!" he shouted.

City hall trembled, the high steeple of St. Philips Church swayed, and winds sounding like a hundred locomotives smashed onto Meeting Street, King Street, Water Street, and the South Battery. Then the mighty storm snaked its way to East Bay and Market streets. The walls of the Charleston Paper Company building bulged outward and the roof collapsed. Masonry columns supporting the heavy slate roof of the old market gave way, crushing more than a dozen people. Docks at the Charleston Shipbuilding and Drydock Company were destroyed.

A lesser storm had now crashed onto the peninsula and damaged the Carolina Yacht Club and Clyde Line terminal. North of the city, two more tornadoes were touching down here and there, teasing frightened people who were crouching under furniture in hope of saving their lives.

By half past eight, all was quiet. And then came the sirens, as every available nurse and physician went to the injured. Marines and sailors from the Navy Yard, troops from Fort Moultrie, and marines from Parris Island rushed to the stricken city. Hundreds of WPA (Work Projects Administration) workers came to help. From the air the paths of the tornadoes were tracked. It was sheer devastation.

A hole gaped in the roof of St. Michael's Church. The fourth floor of a hotel had disappeared. The old Confederate Home on Broad Street was wrecked. Mrs. Ravenel's old haunt, the Fort Sumter Hotel, was

damaged. Not a window remained in the city hall building. Automobiles were overturned and some had been tossed through store windows.
Hundreds of people were injured, and thirty-two were dead.

"The Day of the Tornadoes," as that day is now called, yielded up an
unexpected surprise. As the city, aided by funds from the federal government, began to rebuild, a crew was sent to a shattered house on Price's
Alley. It was the home of Payne, the man Mrs. Ravenel had referred to
as "that effeminate man, the photographer." As they searched the basement, they saw that a filing cabinet had fallen over during the storm.
Under the filing cabinet lay a gun. When a bullet was found in the
chamber, Detective Herman Berkman was called to take a look.

"It's a .38-caliber, all right," the officer remarked. "And the copper-
jacketed bullet has been hand-filled. It's a dead ringer for the weapon
that killed Mrs. Ravenel."

The gun was sent to the F. B. I. for tests, but it was so badly damaged
by saltwater that no positive identification could be made. Regardless
of what the tests proved, Dectective Berkman was convinced that
Payne had murdered Mrs. Ravenel. But with no evidence, and the more
pressing matters of the storm cleanup to consider, the Ravenel murder was left officially unsolved.

But, in spite of the lack of "official" evidence, was the murder really solved that day? You decide.

Vengeance Is Mine

We have a lot of people here who just do nothing but lay up and play sports. These guys have it made—three meals a day, no worries in the world. There can never be any kind of reform like this.

There are plenty of islands, such as a desert island 650 miles from Tahiti. Just send life-term and death inmates there, myself included. I've got twenty-three people ready to leave tomorrow. Once or twice a year, medical supplies could be dropped in. The place wouldn't have to be guarded. We could farm, grow the food we eat, and it would save the state millions of dollars.

Mass murderer Donald "Pee Wee" Gaskins

Outside it was dark and lonely as Myrtle Moon counted the day's receipts just prior to closing Moon's Exxon. It was March 18, 1978, and as he usually did around half past nine each night, Bill Moon was helping his wife close up their small grocery store located four miles from Murrells Inlet, South Carolina.

Moon had spent twenty years in the air force as a military policeman. He had trained guard dogs, and he looked tough. But Moon was a kind man who sometimes gave unemployed neighbors a loaf of bread or a quart of milk without adding it to their bill. In addition to running the convenience store, Moon was also studying criminal justice at nearby Coastal Carolina College in his spare time. On this fateful day, Bill was fifty; his wife Myrtle was forty-eight.

Myrtle and Bill were about halfway through their usual close-up-shop routine when an arrogant young man carrying a .12-gauge shot-gun burst through the door. The eyes of Rudolph Tyner, an eighteen-year-old kid from Harlem who had stolen a car so he could drive to the South, went straight to the bills being turned and straightened in Myr-tle Moon's hands. He glanced out into the dark night. Tyner knew his lookout would yell if anyone approached.

A cryptic grin spread across Tyner's face as he assessed Bill Moon. This was not going to be as easy as Tyner had planned. He had thought they would be scared and just hand over the money. But Bill Moon didn't look scared. Maybe a shot in the arm would make him look a lit-tle more frightened. Tyner took aim, pulled the trigger. The small building shook from the foundation. The bullet not only scared Bill Moon but killed him on the spot.

When Myrtle Moon saw her husband fall, she began to scream hys-terically. Calmly, Tyner took aim and shot her as well. As she fell to the floor, he scooped up around two hundred dollars and fled into the night to join his accomplice, Carl Davis, who was just seventeen.

Shortly after the shooting, one of Moon's daughters wandered into the store with a teen-aged friend to buy Pepsis and candy. Seeing the Moons lying in pools of blood, they ran out of the building, screaming in panic.

Across the road, Tony Cimo was lying on a couch in his trailer, watching John Wayne in *Rio Lobo*. If ever there was a man who loved his parents, it was Tony. He was two when his mother married Bill Moon. It was a young family, the parents being only nineteen then. But Bill Moon had been a good father to Tony. Myrtle and Bill also had three daughters, and their family had always been a close one.

After Moon's retirement from the air force, he ran a seafood restau-rant. When the restaurant became too much work, Bill decided to pur-chase a small grocery store. Bill also urged Tony, his wife Jan, and their two daughters to move from Atlanta to Murrells Inlet. Tony and his family could help in the store, escape urban crime, and be near their family all with this one move. Bill was a strong if gentle persuader, and the move was made. With all the family together, there were happy times of family outings and dinners at the picnic table in back of the Moon house. Tony was second only to Bill Moon as head of the family, and the picnic table became a frequently used family gathering place. After Tony was involved in a serious boating accident, Moon helped support Tony and his family until he recovered. The family was more than close, they were a unit living in harmony.

The piercing shrieks of his sister jarred Tony from the John Wayne movie. Something must have happened at the grocery store, he thought. Tony raced to the scene and found a nightmare. He would later say, "I looked over the counter and my mother and father were laying in a pool of blood. My mother had a hole in her chest big enough to stick my fist through. I felt her pulse, but she didn't have any. Neither did my dad. All I could feel was my own heart pounding. The cash register was open."

When Tony noticed a spent shell, he picked it up absently. Why? Why had his parents been killed? Although Bill Moon kept a pistol beneath the counter, he had always advised his family to treat robbers gingerly, to hand over cash, and cooperate during any robbery. Somewhere deep within Tony, violence was smoldering.

Someone had seen a young black man in the grocery store, and Tony had also seen him near his trailer earlier in the evening. Was he the murderer? If so, he probably would still be in the region. Tony flew out to his pickup and sped on surrounding back roads searching for the killer.

Later that night, police arrested Tyner after receiving a tip that a kid from New York had been causing trouble. Tyner was haughty and insolent when he was taken to the station and strip-searched. The police read him his rights five times to make certain he understood he could remain silent. But when a spent shotgun shell fell from his pocket, Tyner began to talk and acknowledged that he had been in the store that night. Police also found two hundred dollars in cash, as well as a shotgun later proved to be the one used in the slaying.

According to those who knew him, Tyner had always been a troubled boy. His mother, a cleaning woman at the Empire State Building, said Rudolph suffered brain damage at birth and that his IQ was only eighty. Tyner dropped out of seventh grade, which was no surprise since he frequently skipped school and made poor grades. Tyner's brother Archibald said that Rudolph did not get along very well with children his own age and always ran with an older crowd.

The eight women and four men who sat on the jury at Tyner's trial first heard the taped confession that Tyner had made on the night of the murder. Tyner countered by saying he felt threatened by the police when he was arrested, so he had confessed. The defense attorney pointed out that Tyner was mentally retarded and that it was impossible for him to fully understand his rights.

At the close of the trial, the circuit solicitor, Donald Myers, made a final statement referring to the defendant: "You don't take the law into your own hands." He went on to say that one person isn't the judge, jury, and executioner and that Tyner was guilty of one of the most barbarous crimes ever to be committed on the coast of South Carolina. His words were powerful, and the jury didn't ignore them.

Shortly before the circuit judge, Paul Moore, delivered his instructions to the jury, Tyner, dressed in a blue suit and wearing a small cross on a metal chain around his neck, made his own speech to the jury.

"Ladies and gentlemen, I know I made a mistake," Tyner said. "For God's sake, please have mercy on me. That is all I can say. Thank you."

Judge Moore then told the jury members that if they found Tyner guilty they had a choice of whether to vote unanimously for life in prison or unanimously for the death penalty. "You have no enemies to punish; you have no friends to reward."

In the end, Tyner's confession played an integral part in the jury's conclusion. They found Tyner guilty of killing William B. Moon and his wife Myrtle. They also recommended the death penalty, and Tyner was sentenced to die in the state's electric chair on August 16, 1978. The case was automatically appealed to the state supreme court, but Tony Cimo and his family went home and started living their lives again, believing justice had been served.

A year later, Tony heard some news on the radio that shook him to his toes. The South Carolina Supreme Court had ordered a new trial for Tyner, based on the grounds that prosecutors biased jurors by telling them any death sentence would be reviewed automatically. What kind of legal double talk was this? Tyner was guilty of murder!

"That was the beginning of our disillusionment with the court system," said Rene Guyton, one of the Moons' daughters. "We suddenly realized there was no death penalty in South Carolina. No one would ever be killed." The death penalty had not been enforced since the last execution had taken place in 1962. In 1977, the state's penalty law had been declared unconstitutional because it provided no separate sen-

tencing procedure. Many of the prisoners in Columbia who were awaiting execution were now in a state of limbo. All of those death row
inmates worried Tony. How long would it take for justice to be served
on Tyner? The idea of a new trial for Tyner was downright disgusting.

The family gathered at the picnic table in the backyard of their parents' house, the scene of so many family get-togethers, to discuss the
latest developments. There had been countless times of laughter, teasing, and serious planning for the future around that table. Now they
were all weeping. Everyone was devastated at the thought of another
trial. "I can't go through it again, Tony," cried one of Tony's sisters.

Tony was a physically powerful man, but he was also gentle, and no
one in his family had ever seen him out of control with anger. But the
murders, the trial, and the long wait for the execution had turned his
insides into a volatile mix of gunpowder. The order for a new trial was
the fuse that finally set him off. He seemed to explode. He punched
a flower pot. He smashed his fist through a door. He bellowed out a series of angry questions. Was Tyner *ever* going to get what was coming
to him? Why was it taking so long? Did no other person in the world
realize what this family was going through? Finally, Tony walked into
the woods to be by himself and think. And the insidious thought came
to him. *I'll have to take care of it myself!*

"I started looking for shady characters and outlaws," he said later.
Tony went to a strip of lounges and bars on U.S. 501 leading into Myrtle Beach, and then to others located downtown. He chatted with bik-
ers, punks, anyone who looked like an ex-con, someone who would
know how to reach all the way to death row.

His friends understood his mission. "There comes a time when a
man has to take things into his own hands for peace of mind," said
Winston Perry, a bait shop operator near Tony's home.

In April 1980 at the Horry County Courthouse in Conway, jurors
were being selected for the second trial of Rudolph Tyner when the
judge granted a transfer to Marion County because he believed the
defendant could not get a fair trial in Horry County. The move was unexpected. Jury selection started all over again for the third trial. More
waiting, Tony agonized. What kind of people did those who had the
power and authority to administer justice think the Moon family were?
Sheep? A meek, unimaginative lot, easily led on and on with no conclusion in sight?

Tony was red-hot as he stormed through the courtroom door at the
new trial. Tyner was brought to the door where Tony was standing. His

hands were handcuffed and two deputy sheriffs flanked him. The prisoner looked at Tony and smiled, his eyes glowing like a fox's deep in the woods. Suddenly Tony attacked him. "I hit him a glancing blow and police were all over me," Tony said later. "I was about to give up when he looked at me and *laughed*. That's when I shoved a cop back and kicked him pretty good between the legs. Broke my ring finger before deputies wrestled me down."

Tyner was not seriously injured, but he did receive cuts on the cheek and ear, and a torn coat. A deputy sheriff's hand was injured. Tony Cimo and Dean Guyton, his brother-in-law, were held in county jail overnight by order of the judge.

Finally, in October 1980, the jury in Marion County began deliberations. The judge sent them home on a Friday evening at ten o'clock, and they returned on Saturday morning at nine to continue deliberations. Although Tyner did not take the stand in his own defense, Dr. Harold Morgan, a psychiatrist who examined Tyner several months earlier, testified he found no hard evidence of organic problems but did find a personality disorder. Despite this evidence, Tyner was sentenced to die in the electric chair. However, the state supreme court still had to review the case.

By this time, Jan Cimo had noticed a change in her husband. "In the middle of the night I'd wake up and he wouldn't be in bed," she said. "He'd be sitting out in the den where his mama kept pictures of the family on the wall. He'd be staring at the pictures out there."

Tony Cimo was a study in diverse moods as he combed bars and lounges searching for a go-between. One day he found such a man. Someone from Conway knew an inmate in Central Correctional Institute. Tony smiled oddly as he thought, *we're almost there now*. Word of Tony's intent was sent to the inmate, Gerald McCormick. Word came back that McCormick knew the perfect hit man. He was Donald "Pee Wee" Gaskins, a cagey, squirrel-faced man with a long criminal record, including rape and murder.

Tony had heard of Gaskins. He especially remembered the case of thirteen-year-old Kim Gelkins. Kim's family reported her missing in September 1975. Charleston police quickly opened an investigation. Information came in bits and pieces, most of them including the name of Gaskins. Officials eventually were led by one of Gaskins's accomplices to an area where eight bodies were uncovered. Kim Gelkins's body was not among the first eight, but when her remains were found, another body was discovered about a quarter of a mile away. From December 1975 to April 1978 thirteen murdered corpses buried in im-promptu backwoods graves were uncovered. Some of the victims had been killed as early as 1970, and most had been murdered in pairs. All the deaths were linked to one man—Pee Wee Gaskins.

Gaskins was charged in seven of these deaths, and on May 28, 1976, he was convicted and sentenced to die for the murder of one of them. The sentence was commuted to life in prison following the 1977 rul-ing that the state's capital punishment statute was unconstitutional.

In April 1978, when prosecutors were attempting to put him on death row, Gaskins, facing a possible death sentence, decided to talk. He confessed to killing seven of the victims buried in Florence County. Gaskins also led authorities to the graves of his murdered niece, fifteen-year-old Janice Kirby, and Patricia Ann Allsbrook, who had disap-peared together in 1970. All in all, Gaskins was given nine life terms for murder.

Tony Cimo considered the sordid details of Gaskins's crimes and found some irony in the fact that Gaskins was only around to be his hit man because of the same ruling that had kept Tyner from the electric chair. A convicted murderer would kill a convicted murderer. Well, there was a certain amount of poetic symmetry in that.

Tony and Gaskins plotted their scheme during Sunday morning tele-phone calls. Tony placed the calls at a friend's house to keep them from being traced to his place. At first, Gaskins asked for poison, and after some research Tony came up with the idea of using oleander leaves. "They said one leaf from an oleander bush would be enough to kill a child," Tony later recounted. And oleander bushes were certainly plentiful in the coastal region. They were a part of the landscaping in most yards, and besides that, the state highway department used them for decorative plantings. Tony collected some leaves, boiled them down, and mailed the residue to Gaskins, who sprinkled it on Tyner's food. Tyner became nauseous, weak, and pale. When Tony heard this he figured he had scored a triumph. And what was even better, he thought, was that no finger of suspicion would ever be pointed at him. But it wasn't long before Tyner regained his health and was saying, "Give me a Pepsi-Cola and a pack of Kools. And a can of Viennas."

When it became obvious that the oleander poison wasn't working, Tony smuggled cyanide and strychnine in to Gaskins. But Gaskins changed his plan. "You get me a damn stick of dynamite and an elec-tric blasting cap, and we'll put that damn thing in a radio so when he turns it on, it'll blow him into hell and there won't be no coming back on that."

While Tony was trying to round up the explosives, Gaskins somehow came up with the materials himself. Gaskins had the components with which to blow Tyner to kingdom come, and Tony didn't even know it. Nor did he realize that Gaskins had recorded the telephone conversations between the two of them. Gaskins had agreed to murder Tyner for money, but he also was planning to blackmail Tony into paying him even more money.

The cells of Gaskins and Tyner stood back to back. The Civil War-era cells were like cages and among the ugliest and most primitive of those in any prison. Being cooped up in such a nasty vault was not pleasant, and prisoners welcomed any outlet for recreation. One day Gaskins whispered to Tyner that he was going to rig up a device through which they could talk back and forth. Gaskins had been sneaking him food and drugs, and he was one of the few who had gained Tyner's confidence. Tyner looked forward to a communication system between the two cells. Talking to Pee Wee would be a pleasant diversion.

James Brown, another CCI convict, frequently made deliveries of food, drugs, and other items to death row inmates. One day Gaskins asked him to give Tyner a blue plastic cup, like the ones commonly used in the cafeteria. Brown didn't know that this one had been packed with explosives, but he noticed a small speaker in the cup. Later, when Brown saw Gaskins running a wire from a vent in his cell across a utility passageway and through a vent into Tyner's cell, he felt that something fishy was going on, but said nothing.

When the rigging was finished, Tyner grabbed the speaker and held it to his ear. He thought he would hear Gaskins's voice as soon as he plugged the cord into the electrical outlet. Tyner pushed it in. When the wire made contact, the plastic explosive detonated, blowing away one of Tyner's hands and a portion of his head. Tony Cimo heard the news on the radio. He was flabbergasted. Where had Pee Wee gotten the explosives to kill Tyner?

Gaskins was considered a suspect immediately. His cell was searched, and the tape recordings, revealing the telephone conversations between Pee Wee and Tony, were found. On the tapes was a discussion of attempts to poison Tyner and plans for a fatal explosion.

One of the most appalling things about the whole affair was that Pee Wee Gaskins apparently had the run of his entire cell block. Not only did he have the freedom to mastermind the death of a fellow inmate, but to amass the materials to be used in a fatal bombing. Although the inmates in the cell blocks within CCI often were resourceful and cunning, they needed "outside" help in collecting munitions and other substances necessary in carrying out a criminal endeavor—and they got it. Gaskins somehow received the explosives. An attorney would later explain, "It could have been mailed. A visitor could have brought it. It could have been passed over a fence. I have no nagging thoughts about it because I know it wouldn't have been difficult to get it in."

Sam McCuen, a prison spokesman, agreed. "Plastics is the most innocent looking material you've ever seen in your life. As big as a stick of chewing gum. You could walk through La Guardia airport with a piece of it stuck to your nose and no one would notice it. And it would take just about that much of it to do the [desired] damage."

The taped telephone conversations outlining the plot to kill Tyner were admitted as evidence during the opening session of Pee Wee Gaskins's murder trial. After the tapes were played in open court, twelve Richland County citizens decided that confessed mass murderer Donald Gaskins should die in South Carolina's electric chair. Then the question came up of where to keep him while awaiting execution.

"The prisoners over on death row don't want him around," corrections department spokesman Sam McCuen said. "They're scared of him." There also was reason for concern about Gaskins's own safety. As the word of Tyner's murder spread through the prison grapevine, inmates turned on Gaskins. He was taken to the Maximum Security Center where someone could keep an eye on him.

Tony had actually pleaded guilty to misprison of a felony (not reporting a crime of which he was aware); threatening the use of explosive devices; and conspiracy to commit murder.

A stream of character witnesses had taken the stand to talk about what could happen to a solid citizen who finally couldn't take it anymore. Tony's family, co-workers, and friends joined the Horry County sheriff, M. L. Brown, Jr., and the circuit solicitor, Jim Dunn, in speaking on Tony's behalf. Through their testimony, they re-created a four-year nightmare that finally drove Tony to a desperate and criminal act. He was described by friends and lawyers as a man driven by grief, and manipulated by Pee Wee Gaskins.

Ansel Blanton, a fellow construction worker who felt his friend had been tormented by what he felt was justice too slow in being delivered, said, "I think he's getting the shaft if he serves one day."

Cimo again defended his action and said he hoped it helped change public opinion about the legal system. "I hope it might open up some eyes," he said. "I hope that everybody tries to get even with the system, but I hope they try to do it with the legislature."

Richard Harpootlian, the former deputy fifth circuit solicitor, had another version of the ordeal. The vigilante-hero version of Cimo "is a bunch of crap," he said. "Cimo's the guy who associated with, contracted with the most notorious murderer in the state to blow up a man in a cage. There's nothing to admire in that act. He [Tyner] would have been executed, and whether he is to be executed or not is not for Tony Cimo to decide."

Tony Cimo, the thirty-seven-year-old Murrells Inlet family man who had no prior convictions before he pleaded guilty to conspiracy to commit murder, received a total of twenty-one years in prison. For the first two crimes, he received eight-year sentences, and five years for the third. Because the sentences were to be served concurrently, Tony was eligible for parole after serving about a third of the lengthiest term.

Before passing sentence, the circuit judge, James Morris, told Cimo, "Even though I do not sympathize [with your action] or approve of your action, I can understand it." Morris went on to say, "We cannot have people taking the law into their own hands. If we condoned that, there would be a possibility that others would do the same thing."

A whirlwind of national media attention had spotlighted Tony for months, but on June 23, 1983, he was scheduled to trade his new celebrity status for life as a convict. "I'm kind of dreading it," Tony told reporters as he kissed his wife and family good-bye. Holding a beer, he finally climbed into a friend's truck for the 175-mile drive to the Richland County Judicial Center. His wife Jan said that by noon she and Cimo's two daughters "got the tears out of our system. We started counting the time until he returns home."

Tony Cimo was a model prisoner during his time in jail and was never considered a danger to society. By all accounts, he was an ideal candidate for the Department of Corrections' work-release program. He served less than six months of his prison term before he went into the work-release program. Under that procedure he spent nights and weekends in a minimum-security facility near Florence. After serving less than three years of his sentence, Tony Cimo was paroled.

We are all left to wonder who is the good, who is the bad, and what evil was worked in the name of justice. Tony Cimo had a death row inmate killed, something the state of South Carolina seemed unable to do. Was it justice, or was it vengeance?

Cimo expresses no regrets, "I dreamed constantly about him laughing while my mother begged on her knees for her life. . . . Plain as the TV, I kept seeing my mother and father lying in a pool of blood. . . . I feel better knowing he's dead. . . . I don't feel the good Lord holds nothing against me for this. . . . I'd do it again."

Deadly Combination

The black Blazer pulling out of the parking lot of the apartment complex near Guilford College was a moving time bomb. Not only was the van wired with explosives, but inside was a small arsenal. Among the weapons were two Ithaca lightweight shotguns, an Israeli Uzi, a .45-caliber semiautomatic pistol, a .308-caliber assault rifle with a bipod, a flare gun, gas masks, several kinds of knives, a machete, brass knuckles, handcuffs, choke wires, smoke grenades, flares, martial arts armament, and cyanide tablets.

Several unmarked police cars were following at a distance. A State Bureau of Investigation plane circled overhead. Also in pursuit was a SBI car. Detective Allen Gentry of the Forsyth County Sheriff's Department told squad leader Tommy Dennis that they had their felony suspect for the three murders under investigation in the Blazer ahead, traveling north.

Unexpectedly, lightning illuminated the scene—the black Blazer, the caravan of police vehicles following, the masklike faces of the participants, the black clouds looming over it all like some giant pterodactyl. The sudden lightning bolt made the scene seem even more terrifying and surreal.

Inside the Blazer everything was out of focus, ghostly. Fritz Klenner was driving the van. His facial muscles were tight and intense with apprehension. In the front passenger seat was Susie Newsom Lynch, her body immobile, her face a stony mask. Crouched in the back seat were her two sons, John and Jim, holding on to Showie and Maizie, their dogs. How did things ever get this far out of hand?

Susie Newsom Lynch was a member of one of North Carolina's most noted families. Her mother had been a Sharp, and there were dozens who trusted the Sharps right after the Almighty. Stories were told of the Sharps that showed a deep respect which went back for generations. Susie Lynch's aunt, for whom she was named, had become a lawyer and joined her father's practice in Reidsville. After distinguishing herself in that field, Susie Sharp became the first female superior court judge in North Carolina, and she was respected by lawyers across the state. "Judge Susie," as she was affectionately called, always walked regally to the judges' chambers, her black robes flowing, and at least one lawyer who tried his cases at her bench brought roses from his garden to cheer her. Not only was she worthy of the respect she had garnered over the years, but she also had more than a full measure of natural beauty. As time went on, Judge Susie became the first woman in America to be elected chief justice of a state supreme court. Lawyers found her honest and fair, and some of them said that when she spoke, stars and stripes rose right up to the sky.

Judge Susie's youngest sister Florence had married Robert W. Newsom, Jr., in 1945. Florence taught school, and Robert worked at R. J. Reynolds Tobacco Company. When their first child was born on Christmas Eve of 1946, the little girl was named Susie Sharp Newsom in honor of Judge Sharp.

Judge Susie's other sister, Annie Hill, would also play an important role in the life of Susie Newsom. While earning a degree in nursing at Duke University, Annie met and married a promising young doctor, Fred Klenner. When their son Fritz was born, no one could have known that the lives of Fritz and his first cousin, Susie Newsom, would someday become so intricately interwoven.

Even though they were members of a prominent, relatively wealthy family, Susie and her younger brother Robert were raised on a farm because their father didn't want them to grow up in the city. They had ponies and other animals, and Susie had a special knack with them. She loved history and devoured historical fiction and nonfiction, particularly anything about the Orient.

Susie was conservative—both in politics and in religion—and the sixties came and went without her ever getting caught up in the turbulence of the times. She was a good student and an obedient daughter.

Somewhere along the way, Susie developed an unbending attitude toward life. She believed some mistakes—being wrong, doing wrong—were irredeemable and unforgivable. She began to carry lifelong grudges against people for the smallest offenses, in her mind unpardonable. Her God was a judgmental one, but Susie believed that was as it should be. And in her mind, she was never wrong or at fault because to be so would be unforgivable.

Susie enrolled at Queens College in Charlotte and made good grades. But she was somewhat shy and Queens was "too social" for her taste, so she transferred to Wake Forest University. It was during her junior year there that Susie met and fell in love with Tom Lynch.

During all these years Susie was close to the aunt for whom she was named, and their times together raced by all too quickly. It seemed that almost before they turned around twice, the young Susie was ready for marriage.

On the day of her wedding to Tom Lynch in 1970, Susie Newsom got off to a bad start with her mother-in-law. Before the ceremony, the bride found fault with the dress of her sister-in-law, Janie Lynch. The mother of the groom became miffed at the bride's critical attitude, and there was a disagreement. Complications from this clash were so deep-seated that the grudges would extend for years. During the next four years while Tom was in dental school at the University of Kentucky in Lexington, Tom and Susie drove to Prospect, Kentucky, only once to visit his family, only eighty-five miles away.

By 1974 Tom had received a commission in the Naval Reserve, and he and Susie moved to Beaufort, South Carolina, near the marine training center at Parris Island. To the outsider, Beaufort is a community of affluence, taste, and cultivation. Many large and elaborate houses, designed in "the Beaufort style" for airiness and coolness, line the streets of the old city at Port Royal Sound. It wasn't surprising that a girl of Susie's background found the gentility of Beaufort pleasing, and it was there that she and Tom were blessed with the birth of their first child, John.

Shortly after the baby's birth, Tom's mother called her daughter-in-law to let her know they were in town. Tom was at work when the call came. Obviously thinking back on the quarrel with her mother-in-law on the day of her wedding, Susie advised Delores Lynch to get a motel room and call the next day for an appointment to see the child. Delores was upset. She visited her daughter-in-law and grandson, and then she left for home. A deeper chasm now divided the two women. On March 26, 1976, another son, Jim, was born to Susie and Tom. It would be a year before Delores would lay eyes on Jim.

When Tom's discharge came through, he decided to practice dentistry in Albuquerque, New Mexico, in the heart of the American Southwest. Although that area is called "the Land of Enchantment" because of the beauty of the region and the history of the people, no place could be more different from the Old South that Beaufort typified.

The Lynch family soon moved into a pueblo house, something foreign to the landscape of the southern coastal plain. Susie despised the place, complaining that there was no culture in Albuquerque. She became angry and unhappy and blamed Tom for both. He argued that there *was* culture there, it was just different from that of the Southeast. After all, he pointed out, the southwestern Indians lived in pueblos, built of stucco over a frame, as early as 1540.

Just as Spanish and Indian architecture influenced construction in New Mexico, the foods of that area were also different from those in the Southeast. Red chili peppers, hanging on strings from porch rafters, drying in the intense sun after the autumn harvest in the Rio Grande Valley, were common. Staples in most family diets consisted of chili con carne, sopapillas and tostadas. Susie hated the food, too, and arguments with Tom became more frequent and more virulent.

After three years, Susie was confiding her unhappiness to friends. In January 1979 she piled her two sons into her Audi Fox and left New Mexico forever. When she reached North Carolina, she called Tom and told him that she would not be returning. A separation agreement was eventually drawn up that gave Susie full custody of the children.

After returning to North Carolina, Susie revived her old interest in Far Eastern culture. She met a Taiwanese student at Guilford College who could teach her Mandarin, and against the wishes of Tom and her parents, Susie took her children to Taiwan soon after Christmas.

Again Susie found herself in surroundings which were so alien and remote she could barely accept them. Cockroaches ran up the walls of her tiny abode, and the thought of germs all but nauseated her. Although the move hadn't been what she hoped for, she decided to tough it out in order to do research about the country and its management and administration, research which she planned to use to get a degree in anthropology. She continued to work in the poverty-stricken and cheerless surroundings—teaching English in the mornings, taking Chinese classes in the afternoons, and getting supper for herself and the boys in the evenings.

In less than six months she'd had enough, and on June 25, 1980, Susie and her sons boarded a plane for home. Although she was pleased to be leaving Taiwan behind and to be starting over again, she didn't realize her life was changing in another way as well. Tom had started divorce proceedings that same day.

On her journey home, Susie did take the time to visit with her mother-in-law at the airport in Chicago. Delores hugged her grandsons and found her reunion with Susie friendlier than she had expected. However, Susie wasn't in robust health, and by the time she arrived home in North Carolina, she was exhausted, pale, and lacked energy. Her mother Florence urged her to visit her uncle, Dr. Fred Klenner, in Reidsville. He incorrectly diagnosed the problem as multiple sclerosis and prescribed massive doses of B vitamins. While making medical visits to her uncle, Susie became reacquainted with her cousin, Fred Jr., whom everyone called Fritz.

Susie had heard that Fritz was strange, but she wondered why some of the other cousins felt that way about him. She didn't think he was odd. In fact, she liked him.

Fritz's father, Dr. Fred Klenner, was a well-known doctor who had received national attention for his treatments using vitamin C. Even Dr. Linus Pauling, a Nobel Prize-winning chemist, had called attention to Dr. Klenner's work in his book, *Vitamin C and the Common Cold*.

Dr. Klenner was the town eccentric, and most folks in Reidsville thought that was just fine. His patients adored him, not minding that he was completely out of touch with contemporary life. He maintained separate waiting rooms for blacks and whites until his death and continued to use old-fashioned sterilizers instead of the disposable needles every other doctor in the country employed.

His philosophy, devoutly and passionately incorporated into the very thread of his life, was a strange and bubbling moral quagmire. Dr. Klenner believed that communists had infiltrated all levels of government, that UFOs regularly visited earth, that the National Rifle Association could govern the country better than elected officials, that Armageddon was at hand. His religion was closer to medieval Catholicism than to anything seen in the last two centuries, and he and Fritz wore scapulars and talked of omens and portents.

In fact, Fritz bought into most of his father's beliefs. Nevertheless, Fritz was as well loved by his father as Dr. Klenner was by his patients, and his boyhood seemed perfectly normal to him.

Fritz and his father had been best friends since Fritz was a baby, and both wanted to keep it that way. It would be difficult to picture this father scolding his son or telling him to wash his face or get a haircut. Although few chums called on Fritz at the family home on Huntsdale Drive in Reidsville, he was able to entertain himself with the things his father amassed in their house—books and journals and art and various medical equipment. Among the collections displayed in the house was an assemblage of guns. Fritz was charmed by the guns in much the way one is fascinated with snakes. Dr. Fred noticed the interest, and when Fritz was in the seventh grade, he gave his son a German Luger as a gift.

It was only natural that Fritz wanted to be near his father, so he began to help his dad out at the clinic. The people who went to Dr. Klenner's clinic for treatment also gave Fritz special attention, and the consideration he received there attracted him to the place. He began to wear a white doctor's coat, and he adopted some of the mannerisms of a physician. As time went on, the patients would joke with Fritz that one day he would become their doctor and take care of them.

In 1970 Fritz became a pre-med student at the University of Mississippi. His father was pleased with the choice. But four years later, when his class graduated, Fritz was not awarded a degree. He announced to his father that he lacked only a few hours, which could be made up during summer school. Although he enrolled in summer school that year, he still did not receive a degree. That fall he signed up for a correspondence course to finish his college work.

At Christmas, Fritz announced he had graduated, and his father was ecstatic. He believed his son was well on his way to becoming a physician, one who would join him at his clinic. However, Dr. Klenner couldn't help but notice that no diploma arrived from Ole Miss. Fritz finally explained that "enemies" at the university had prevented his graduation. Any anxiety that his father experienced was erased in late 1976 when Fritz declared his intention to attend Duke Medical School. *Duke Medical School!* All was wonderful.

Spring came, and Fritz rented an apartment near the Duke campus. Every Monday morning he would leave his home in Reidsville and return there on Friday. Weekends were spent helping his father in the clinic. People were beginning to refer to Fritz as "young Dr. Klenner," but his accounts of his schooling at Duke were hazy, almost like reflec-

tions of characters on the surface of a pool. He told more and more unbelievable accounts of his progress. Still, he was taken at his word by
most people. He spoke of his friends in Durham and their activities,
and all of it sounded legitimate. However, things in Durham were not
as they were being recounted in Reidsville.

In December 1978 Fritz married a schoolteacher, Ruth Dupree. Each
Monday morning he left their apartment in Reidsville and went to
Durham where he said he attended classes. But instead of hobnobbing
with young doctors, Fritz was hanging around a gun shop where survivalist types congregated and at a garage where people worked on su-
perchargers. Standing amidst the machine-gun blasts of pneumatic
wrenches and the sleazy-looking guys in leather jackets fretting around
cycles, Fritz would sometimes wear a white doctor's coat with a stetho-
scope in his pocket. But it was only a fantasy. Now and then he would
casually mention a confidential research accident in which he had become ill, or an encounter with radioactive materials that had killed two
other scientists. Drifting further from reality, he even began to talk
about the FBI. Behind his back, the people in the gun shops, garages,
and the army-navy stores were starting to call him "Dr. Crazy" and
"upper-class weirdo."

Eventually, someone made inquiries at Duke and discovered that
Fritz had never been a student there. One of his wife's friends poked
around, and illegal drugs, syringes, and various medical devices which
Fritz used to aid in the deception that he was a physician were found
among his belongings. Fritz also was toying with cyanide and fashion-
ing poison bullets. Suspicions crept into many minds, and in 1981
when his wife learned the extent of Fritz's deceptions, she left him.

But Fritz wasn't downcast for long. His father bought him a huge,
black, four-wheel-drive Chevrolet Blazer. Before long, Fritz was seen
driving women around town in the black behemoth. He still frequently
mentioned that he was a doctor and spoke of his involvement with the
special forces in Vietnam.

Somehow, Fritz also found time on weekends to help his father in the
clinic. These were some of the best days of their lives, but they were not
to last long. Dr. Klenner fell ill and died on May 20, 1984. Fritz was
devastated, feeling that he had lost a safe harbor, a sure source of comfort, love, and protection. Dr. Klenner's clinic was closed, and Fritz was
crushed. It was at this point that he drew even closer to Susie Lynch.

Fritz had $25,000 from his father's life insurance policy, but it went
fast. He outfitted his vehicle in the grandest survivalist tradition, with

emergency rations, first-aid supplies, guns, and ammunition. The *piece de resistance* was a bomb, bolted to the floor beneath the passenger seat.

That fall, Susie enrolled at Wake Forest University, working toward the desired degree in anthropology. She renewed some old acquaintances and for the first time she could remember in a long while, Susie was having fun.

Meanwhile, Tom, tormented over not seeing his children, was becoming more and more frustrated as he tried to settle the visitation rights issue. After several motions, affidavits, and rulings, it was decreed that he would have his boys for specified times during summer, spring break, and at Christmas. Before Christmas, his divorce was finalized.

But Susie's newly rediscovered relationship with her cousin Fritz was beginning to change. Thoughts of Fritz popped into Susie's mind so frequently that what she had thought was fun at Wake Forest began to fizzle. Before long she dropped her studies there and began taking courses in business at the University of North Carolina at Greensboro. Fritz used the last of his inheritance to help her buy a Blazer S-10. Her parents were concerned—the new influence in Susie's life had not escaped them.

Their concern grew as Susie's hatred and distrust of Tom grew ever more poisonous. They implored her, for the sake of her sons, to reconcile herself to at least a superficially friendly relationship with Tom. Florence pointed out that divorce is usually the fault of both partners and urged her daughter to take an objective look at herself.

Florence's suggestion threw Susie into a towering rage, her wrath way out of proportion to the offense. Susie's philosophy of life did not allow her to accept even the possibility that she might be somehow at fault, or wrong. No, *she* wasn't guilty of unpardonable mistakes. It was Tom. Tom had ruined her life. Couldn't they see that?

Fritz could. He told Susie he had inside information which linked Tom with the mob and drug transactions. Tom was evil, he said, and the failure of the marriage was not Susie's responsibility. It was just what Susie wanted to hear, and she slipped farther away from her family— and from reality.

The issue of Fritz came to a head in January 1983. On the edge of the abyss, Susie moved out of her parents' house and into an apartment complex at Guilford College. In June, her former husband married Kathy Anderson, a woman who had once been his dental assistant. The news arrived at the Guilford College apartment like a bullet.

As Susie rebelled against her family's distrust of Fritz, she was also distancing herself from those who loved her, including her mother, her grandmother, and her aunt. With all of the family turmoil over Fritz, Susie didn't need any more problems.

But it was at this point that Susie received the news which may have pushed her irrevocably over the fine line between mental stability and instability. John and Jim had been visiting their father in Albuquerque. Tom and Kathy loved having the boys, and during previous visits they all went on camping trips or other outings. The boys had mentioned Fritz before, and Tom had worried about the influence Fritz was having on them. But it wasn't until the visit in June 1983 that he became really concerned. The boys seemed withdrawn. They came dressed in camouflage fatigues and talked of guns and killing. They were sick from the megadoses of vitamins Susie sent out with them. When the boys related graphic accounts of Fritz's erratic behavior, Tom in turn told his mother. It was no secret Delores Lynch thought her son hadn't received justice regarding visitation rights anyway, and Tom's news only fueled the flame. After talking to both Delores and Florence, Tom started legal proceedings to get more time with his sons.

The mere thought that Tom might get shared custody rights drove Susie into a frenzy. When she found out Tom's mother was helping him with the exorbitant legal costs, she expressed an almost incomprehensible hatred of Delores to anyone who would listen.

On Tuesday, July 24, 1984, a friend of Delores Lynch tried calling Delores at her Kentucky home to find out why she had missed church Sunday. There was no answer, so she decided to drive over to the comfortable house in Peewee Valley, on Kentucky State Road 329. She had a nagging premonition that something must be wrong. Her eyes were riveted on the house as she approached, but her tense muscles relaxed a bit when she saw three cars parked near the house: the blue Oldsmobile that belonged to Delores, the Volkswagen that had belonged to Delores's husband, who died the previous year, and Janie's Chevrolet Nova. As she drove up, she saw a thirty-foot ribbon of dried blood and the body of Delores, lying lifeless near the cars. She slammed the car into reverse and sped away. Her heart was pounding in her chest as she raced to notify the police.

When the county police chief, Steve Nobles, arrived at the expensive home with white shutters and wrought-iron ornamentation, he examined the body on the concrete. A bullet had entered the back, and a portion of the head and face had been blown away. Janie, who had driven the fifteen miles from Louisville on Sunday to visit her mother, was dead too. Janie's body was found in a room that overlooked the parking area. Apparently she was running from her killer when she, too, had been shot in the back and neck.

Dr. Tom Lynch was just leaving his dental office when an Albuquerque police chaplain came in to tell him the news. A friend accompanied Tom to Kentucky. Every lead was checked, but nothing turned up to pinpoint the killer or killers. It wasn't a robbery; expensive jewelry, money, and valuables were untouched. And a military assault rifle had been used, a mark of a professional hit. The case became more exasperating to the investigators as each hour passed.

John and Jim were in Albuquerque at the time of the murders, and Tom phoned Susie at her apartment and asked if the boys' visit could be extended. He told her his mother and sister had been murdered and he needed the special love his sons could give him. Susie refused the extension. She said she missed her boys and wanted them home with her. She then talked with her lawyer and mentioned that Tom's mother and sister had been murdered in a "gangland killing."

Susie's mother, Florence Sharp Newsom, wrote Tom a five-page, handwritten letter of sympathy. The unbridled hatred and disgust for Tom that she had witnessed in her daughter had not extended to her. Deep down she loved Tom, and her head was spinning as she began the letter that was possibly the beginning of the most defeating and despairing times her family would ever endure. However, she still held on to the belief that Susie would come to her senses and everything would somehow turn out all right for all of them. Tom was pleased to hear from Florence and answered the letter.

In his letters, Tom expressed deep concern for his sons. As a dentist, he was mortified to see that plaque had collected on his own children's teeth. Additionally, he was concerned that they were sleeping on the floor and taking excessive vitamins. There was also a nagging worry about their mental state. Thus began a renewed rapport between Florence and her former son-in-law.

Autumn came and Tom notified Susie that he was coming to North Carolina to visit his sons. This irritated Susie and she went to see her brother Robert. During the conversation she mentioned that Tom was connected to the Mafia. She remarked that she was privy to this information because Fritz was working with the CIA. During the visit, Susie also opened her purse and flashed a gun which she kept inside.

Everybody in the family was now concerned about Susie. There was something so unapproachable about her, a coldness. They were at a loss as to how to deal with it effectively. Judge Susie Sharp met with Susie and made recommendations for the comfort and well-being of the children. Kathy, Tom's wife, was corresponding with Susie in an effort to improve relations with her and subsequently to have more access to the boys. It seemed to be working. Susie was moved by the concern of her family and agreed to go to her parents' home for Christmas. Even her grandmother, Nana, added her touch to a traditional dinner.

Susie had seemed to warm towards her family, but things changed abruptly in March 1985 when Fritz moved from his apartment to hers. With Fritz now living under Susie's roof, they both seemed to slip irrevocably into a neurotic, fantasy-filled world. Susie didn't seem to be upset that Fritz whiled away so many hours in a surplus store in Greensboro, often leaving with hundreds of dollars worth of sleeping bags, knives, and other goods. Fritz was also collecting expensive books on arms and guerrilla warfare. And whenever an occasion arose where he was expected to introduce Susie, Fritz always referred to her as his wife.

By this time John and Jim were not even allowed to write to Tom, and Tom longed to see them, hold them close. Although the boys were planning a trip to Disneyland with Tom and Kathy in April, Tom contacted his lawyer in Reidsville in March 1985 to begin a new campaign for more time with his sons. It was shortly afterwards that Susie learned from her lawyer that her father would be testifying for Tom in the upcoming custody hearing, scheduled for May 23. The lawyer went on to explain that grandparents often were witnesses for opposing sides in custody cases.

At this news, Susie became even more estranged from her parents, whom she considered no better than traitors. She was terrified Tom would be able to take her sons from her, and she repeated her fears to Fritz over and over again. He insisted that he would do the worrying for her, and Susie agreed to let him.

It was around midnight on May 18, 1985, that Detective Allen Gentry took a call from someone saying something about a triple murder. He flew to the house identified by the caller. It was the home of Nana, Susie's grandmother. A storm door had been smashed. In a hallway lay Bob Newsom, Susie's father. He had been shot in the abdomen, right forearm, and head. Items from his wife's purse were scattered near the body. Signs of a battle were all over the living room. A rocker had been overturned, a fireplace set was scattered, and the body of Florence,

Susie's mother, lay nearby. Her wounds were horrible, far more vicious and extensive than mere death required. The only one stabbed, Florence had knife wounds in one lung and her neck, and the aorta was severed and her trachea hacked in two. Nana's body was found on the sofa with a bullet through her temple. She had been covered with an afghan and looked like she was sleeping.

Although robbery at first appeared to be the most obvious motive, the police soon began to question the scenario. How could thieves walk away from expensive jewelry, cash lying in a dish, and other valuables there for the taking?

Detective Gentry took charge of the gruesome murder case and began asking questions. Susie's brother, Rob, mentioned that Susie's mother-in-law and sister-in-law had been murdered a year or so ago in Kentucky and that the murders seemed similar in style.

Word finally got through to Susie about the murders. She seemed strangely detached and mentioned that a dog was missing and she had to search for it. When a friend heard the news and ran to comfort Susie, she was sitting at the kitchen table. All she said was she couldn't believe what she had heard.

Tom was called. He began to put two and two together. His mother and sister had been murdered in Kentucky. His in-laws were murdered in North Carolina. Could the murders be related? Or was it coincidence? As authorities continued to search the Newsom house, they found documents indicating that Susie's father was to appear in court the following week in the custody hearing.

By Sunday night, Susie's brother Rob had collected himself enough to make some deductions of his own. He told the police all his facts and all his fears about Fritz Klenner and his sister's strange and unhealthy dependence on their first cousin. A lawyer, Rob knew it would take days for the police to gather enough evidence to arrest Fritz, so he hid his children with neighbors and friends and tried to get through the next few days. Amidst all the confusion, the funerals still had to be conducted, so he met with Susie to discuss the arrangements.

On Wednesday, when Gentry and SBI agent Tom Sturgill talked with Susie at her apartment, she introduced them to Fritz Klenner. The officers went over the events of the last few days with Susie and Fritz. Susie gave the itinerary for their activities, and they had an alibi for the day of the murders. Fritz was with a friend, Ian Perkins, a student at Washington and Lee University. When Susie was questioned, she was adamant in her assertion that professional murderers had done the job. She mentioned once again that she believed Tom was connected to the mob.

The victims of the Saturday night massacre were buried on Thursday. Susie, Fritz, and the boys arrived in Fritz's black Blazer. After the funeral for Susie's parents, a service was held for Nana. Even at that time, an investigation was going on to try to establish whether or not there was a connection between the murders of Susie's in-laws and her parents and grandmother.

During the week that followed, Gentry and Sturgill went to Susie's apartment again to question Fritz. As he talked, Fritz absent-mindedly pulled his keys from his pocket. Playing with them distractedly, Fritz failed to notice that the officers had detected a handcuff key. Only police were supposed to carry such a key. The conversation came around to Ian Perkins, and the cops mentioned that they planned to go to Lexington, Virginia, to interrogate him.

When the police talked to Ian, they learned that in late 1984 a common interest in intelligence work had brought the two long-time friends even closer. Fritz had visited Ian in Lexington, and they had talked of things they found fascinating. Fritz said, confidentially of course, he had been working for "the agency" for years. He also told Ian he was going to be involved in a "mission" in Texas, and they talked of Ian helping in that venture. (Some people were later to believe that Fritz was thinking of New Mexico rather than Texas.) There was also talk of a job to be done in Winston-Salem and another in Charlotte. Ian was hooked.

Ian explained to the officers that he had assisted Fritz in the CIA operation in Winston-Salem, nothing further. It had nothing to do with the murders in question. The officers asked the student to explain.

On the night of the murders, Ian had driven the Blazer and let Fritz out at a designated location less than a mile from the Newsom home. Fritz was wearing a bulletproof vest and gloves and was carrying a case with two guns and a bayonet in it. He told Perkins his job was to "take out" a dangerous drug smuggler. Ian anxiously awaited Fritz's return, killing time at a local fast-food restaurant. Shortly after midnight, Fritz returned. He was driving a stolen car. The job had been done.

When the officers told Ian that Fritz was neither a doctor nor a CIA operative, he was furious. As the conversation became more revealing, Ian began to see that he had been duped by Fritz.

Another SBI officer joined Gentry and Sturgill on their second visit to Lexington. They told Ian that Fritz had been accused of practicing medicine without a license, that he was dangerous, and that they needed help in connecting him to the murders. Ian agreed to do what he could. A plan was formulated.

Ian didn't know how it would go. It was a crapshoot. He notified Fritz that he was coming to North Carolina and would like to meet him at Penrose Mall.

By the time the Blazer pulled into the parking lot, five surveillance cars had taken up stations around the mall. Ian spoke to the officers before he got into the Blazer. "Say a prayer for me," he whispered into the tiny recorder he was wearing to transmit his conversation with Fritz.

Ian told Fritz that some "cop types" had come to visit him. He went on to say that they were looking into some murders which were committed on the night he had helped Fritz with the CIA job.

Fritz couldn't have been cooler if he had known officers were listening to every word. After the long conversation ended and the officers reviewed it, they decided they needed a clearer, more concise conversation. They asked Ian to try again. The officers coached Ian on the questions he was to ask Fritz the following Sunday. Ian must try to collar Fritz into admitting he had committed the murders. Ian played the planned conversation over in his mind until the very minute he met with Fritz on the second of June.

They sat in the Blazer, which was parked near Zayre's in the O'Henry Shopping Center on Cone Boulevard in Greensboro. Ian told Fritz the officers had shown him the house where the murders were committed. Fritz urged Ian not to worry. "They are just fishing," he said. He told Ian the officers were playing mind games with him.

Ian mentioned that he was scheduled for a polygraph test. Fritz froze. A *lie detector test*. He reached back and pulled a file folder from the back of the van. "There are some pictures in there," he said as he handed the folder to Ian.

Ian looked at the pictures, then closed the folder. He pretended to trust Fritz.

Go on, the officers listening to the conversation were thinking. Admit something. Give us a break.

Suddenly Fritz looked at Ian conspiratorially. In a generous gesture of *esprit de corps*, Fritz confided that he had checked his phone lines and believed they weren't tapped.

He's coming around, the officers thought. But Fritz had not yet given them the headlines they needed.

Then Fritz suddenly spun out a story, saying that he had killed some people. He confided he had knocked off the people in the pictures, although he swore he didn't murder Susie's parents and grandmother.

The officers were pleased that they now had Fritz on tape admitting he had killed some people. But they hadn't yet hit pay dirt. They needed a confession on tape, and they needed it soon. As more time passed, Fritz would have a chance to get suspicious. They'd have to come up with a plan that would push him over the brink—and soon.

On June 3, at eleven o'clock in the morning, Ian Perkins had his third rendezvous with Fritz. Again he was accompanied by a large number of detectives. They had prepared a document which indicated Fritz might be called to be in a police lineup. It was a plot, a scheme to trick Fritz into admitting the murders. Stress had never been greater on Ian. He was nervous, perspiring.

The armed officers moved out of sight. No one would have suspected such a stake-out was taking place. Fritz's Blazer slowly turned into the parking lot in Greensboro.

"Hold on to your seats, gang," Ian said to all who were listening to his recorder. "This is going to be a doozie." He was unaware that he was about to slide into a van which had been wired with explosives.

Almost immediately Fritz started his narrative. He was still maintaining that he was connected to the CIA. Ian interrupted him and mentioned the police lineup. Fritz went pale. If he were to be subjected to a police lineup all his claims about the CIA would be blown sky high. More important, he didn't want to be scrutinized in a row of criminals. There was a barracuda somewhere who knew his innermost fears. He could smell it! Fritz now realized he was cornered. They would be on him any minute now. His mind worked frantically. A bubble of rage burst in his head. He started the motor. Ian jumped out.

As the Blazer left the parking lot, the surveillance cars pulled out to follow. Among those in the ten-mile pursuit to Susie's apartment near Guilford College were Kentucky detectives. They had been called in because they were trying to link Fritz with the murders in their state.

As Fritz arrived at Susie's apartment, the police cars kept back, out of sight. The officers watched Fritz calmly carry items to the Blazer, and they found it surprising to see how much gear he put in the van. Then Susie got in the vehicle. The policemen stared in amazement as she helped her boys, who were dressed in camouflage fatigues, get in the back. Susie called two black dogs, and they too were pulled inside. A call for additional backup was sent out over the police radio. Those hearing the call responded, not knowing what they were in for. Orders regarding the situation were blurted over police car radios. The words were typical for such an emergency.

"That uniform car, come on out Friendly. Be at the exit to Guilford Hills. Rush it up!"

"What do they have out there?"

"Look, we don't want to turn the apartment complex into a shooting gallery. Wait to surround the subject vehicle until it reaches the intersection at . . ."

The drama was now in action. The black Blazer was being chased, and everything was happening so fast almost nothing could be kept straight.

Fritz followed the combat manuals to the letter. He dispassionately responded to the attempt to block his escape route, evading the trap and moving his Blazer in position to fire at his pursuers. Leaning out his window, he calmly sprayed the intersection with the Uzi.

"I've been hurt." It was Tommy Dennis, the squad leader. He was shot in the chest.

"I've been shot!" One of the Kentucky officers called for help.

"All units, three oh three has been shot."

As the caravan moved ahead, led by the Blazer, bullets were going in all directions. The Blazer stopped beyond a curve, and when the chasing cars came into view, Fritz fired on them. Police cars skidded to stops. Men jumped out and ran for cover.

Fritz moved on, never speeding or losing control of the Blazer. The pursuing cars kept back. Officers were frightened. They were dealing with a crazy man. As for Susie, she was sitting immobile through it all. She never turned her head even to look at the converging police cars.

"He's got an automatic weapon," someone screamed as Fritz opened fire.

Suddenly, the brake lights of the Blazer came on and Fritz stopped. He had a police scanner and he had heard the cops talking about the roadblock up ahead. Police cars quickly slowed. The officers didn't know about the scanner then, so they didn't know what Fritz was up to, and they didn't want to be too close.

Just at that moment the officers saw a flurry of activity in the front seat and heard a sputtering sound. And then the Blazer exploded. Parts of it flew as high as the tops of the nearby trees.

"Explosion at one fifty just east of Bronco Lane," a voice said into a microphone. "He just blew the whole thing up. Get an ambulance out here."

The police moved into the circle of acrid smoke, their guns drawn. Fritz was lying face down, but he was still breathing erratically. Susie's body was a crumpled mass entangled with parts of car seats. The boys had died the death of the innocent. They had been given strong doses of cyanide and had lapsed into comas just before they had been fatally shot in the head. By the time the ambulance arrived, Fritz had died.

Just at that moment, the giant thunderstorm that had gathered over the town exploded, forcing the officers back to their cars. The dreadful thunder clapped and roared loudly, and rainwater ran in rivulets as the law enforcement officers sat in their cars, restricted from examining what was left of the Blazer and its occupants. In the midst of the sudden storm came a tempest of hail. But sudden summer storms are short, and it wasn't long before the officers were able to examine the devastation. They searched ruefully beneath a mocking sky, and the scene would burn forever in their minds.

Everyone in the Blazer was wearing a scapular and rosary beads, more evidence of Fritz's influence over their lives. Body parts were flung all across the highway. Susie had been sitting on the bomb, and there wasn't much left of her from the waist down. The thunderstorm left clouds of steam moving over the bodies like a living, breathing shroud. The devastation looked like a scene from hell.

Several years later, it now seems clear that the murders of five women, one man, two children, and two dogs can be credited to Fritz Klenner's account. What isn't clear—and what is still hotly debated—is which of those acts goes on Susie Newsom Lynch's account.

It has been proved that Susie wasn't present at the killing of her parents and grandmother, and most people doubt she was actually present at the Lynch murders. But did she know about the murders in advance? Or did she realize afterwards that Fritz was involved and, by her silence, condone his actions? Or was Susie so mentally unbalanced that she sanctioned the murders on some abstract plane, but was far removed from the reality of it all?

Surely someone as intelligent as Susie would have to notice that when she complained of a problem to Fritz, that "problem" would soon get "fixed." Still, there is little to connect Susie with the actual planning or execution of any of the murders.

Moral responsibility may not be the same thing as legal culpability, but Tom Lynch seems to have decided Susie was *somehow* responsible. In 1987, Tom filed a lawsuit regarding the disposition of the estates of Susie's parents and grandparents. In the lawsuit, Tom accuses his ex-wife of complicity in the murders. Under North Carolina law, that would prevent her from inheriting the estates, estimated at somewhere between $300,000 and $500,000. Since both Susie and her children were dead, Tom, as the administrator of his sons' estate, would control the fortune.

We may never know the whole truth. But we do know that the relationship between Fritz and Susie metamorphasized into something dark and unspeakably malignant. As Rob Newsom now says, "her incipient mental illness meshed so perfectly with his well-developed madness [the situation] grew very sick very quickly." And the combination was every bit as explosive as the bomb that blew them into oblivion. They achieved their own personal Armageddon.

Author's Story Notes

The following story notes indicate some of the sources used by the author in adapting the stories for this book, including published sources consulted and people interviewed. These notes are also intended to give the reader a general overview of some of the author's research, but they are by no means comprehensive.

A Devil of a Beauty

The primary source used in this story was a collection of sermons entitled *The Devil in Petticoats or God's Revenge Against Husband Killing*, by Reverend M. L. Weems. Augusta: Daniel Starnes and Company, 1810.

Poetry on the Gallows

Sources consulted by the author included a paper entitled "Frankie Silver," a paper prepared by attorney S. J. Ervin, Jr., for the Morganton Kiwanis Club, October 28, 1930; and a paper entitled "Frankie Silver" written by Carolyn Sakowski for a graduate course at Appalachian State University, 1972. Several articles from the *News Herald* (Morganton, North Carolina) were also used, including "Recalled Ghosts of Two in Old Tragedy," February 5, 1931; "Legends Have Grown Up about Frankie Silvers," March 27, 1964; and "How Curious Crowd Came for the Hanging," February 13, 1968.

The Woman Who Was Murdered Twice

The primary source used in this story was a collection of sermons entitled *The Devil in Petticoats or God's Revenge Against Husband Killing*,
by Reverend M. L. Weems. Augusta: Daniel Starnes and Company,
1810.

Daddy Dearest

Sources consulted by the author included *The Independent Republic
Quarterly*, edited by Florence Theodora Epps. Horry County Historical Society, April 1971 and Spring 1984; and *The Independent Republic of Horry*, Tricentennial 1670 - 1970, Horry County Historical
Society.

The Man Who Escaped His Own Grave

The primary source used in this story was an article entitled "Killer
Escaped from Grave," by Heath Thomas, which appeared in the *News
and Observer* (Raleigh, North Carolina) on October 3, 1965.

A Love Triangle, Victorian-Style

Material for this story was derived from the following books: *The Dwell-
ing Houses of Charleston, South Carolina*, by Alice R. Huger Smith and
D. E. Huger Smith. New York: Lippincott, 1917; *Famous Houses of
Charleston, South Carolina*, which was a booklet published by the
Charleston News and Courier and the *Evening Post* (Charleston, South

Carolina), 1970; *Charleston Interiors*, by N. Jane Iseley and Henry F. Cauthen, Jr. Charleston: Preservation Society of Charleston, Inc., 1979; and *Charleston Murders* by Samuel A. Cothran, Frank K. Myers, Thomas K. Peck, Samuel Gaillard Stoney, Rowena Wilson Tobias, and Thomas R. Waring, Jr. New York: Duell, Sloan, and Pearce, 1947; and the *Charleston News and Courier*, March 13, 1889.

The author also interviewed Jack Leland, a Charleston journalist, several times and obtained information not contained in the books listed above.

Death at Little Black Creek Swamp

The primary source used in this story was an article entitled, "Murder Near Garner Station," by John G. Duncan, which appeared in the *News and Observer* (Raleigh, North Carolina) on September 10, 1967.

Bad Seed: The Murdering Bighams

Sources consulted by the author included *The Last of the Bighams*, by J. A. Zeigler. Orangeburg, South Carolina: Sandlapper Publishing Company, 1984 (Zeigler, editor of the *Florence Morning News-Review* at the time of the Bigham trials, covered the six-year court proceedings and published his book about the case in 1927.); *A Piece of the Fox's Hide*, by Katharine Boling. Orangeburg: Sandlapper Publishing Company, 1972; "The Bigham Murders," by Ethlyn D. Missroon, *Myrtle Beach Magazine*, Winter, 1986; and articles too numerous to mention, most of which appeared in the *Florence Morning News* (Florence, South Carolina).

Will the Real Murderer Please Stand Up?

The primary source used in this story was an article entitled, "The Diabolical Frame-Up of Joel Levy: Questions Unanswered," by Pat Reese, which appeared in the *Fayetteville Observer-Times* (Fayetteville, North Carolina) on November 28, 1982.

Murder in the Mansion?

Books consulted in researching this story include: *Libby Holman: Body and Soul*, by Hamilton Darby Perry. Boston: Little, Brown and Company, 1983; *Dreams that Money Can Buy*, by Jon Bradshaw. New York: William Morrow and Company, 1985; *Nostalgia Spotlight on the Twenties*, by Michael Anglo. London: Jupiter Books, 1976; *Nostalgia Spotlight on the Thirties*, by Michael Anglo. London: Jupiter Books, 1976; *Time Capsule/1932*, by Henry R. Luce. New York: Time-Life Books, 1968; and *All the Things We Are*, by Louis Tanner. New York: Doubleday, 1968.

Other publications that were used included articles in *The Charlotte Observer* (Charlotte, North Carolina), July 9, 1932 and June 6, 1971; and "1932 Tragedy Still a Mystery," by Linda Griffith, *Greensboro Daily News-Record* (Greensboro, North Carolina), September 28, 1980; and brochures from the Reynolda House in Winston-Salem, North Carolina.

Murder on Meeting Street

Material for this story was derived from the following books: *The Dwelling Houses of Charleston, South Carolina*, by Alice R. Huger Smith and D. E. Huger Smith. New York: Lippincott, 1917; *Famous Houses of Charleston, South Carolina*, which was a booklet published by the

Charleston News and Courier and the *Evening Post* (Charleston, South Carolina), 1970; *Charleston Interiors*, by N. Jane Iseley and Henry F. Cauthen, Jr. Charleston: Preservation Society of Charleston, Inc., 1979; *Charleston Murders*, by Samuel A. Cothran, Frank K. Myers, Thomas K. Peck, Samuel Gaillard Stoney, Rowena Wilson Tobias, and Thomas R. Waring, Jr. New York: Duell, Sloan, and Pearce, 1947; "5 Tornadoes Wrecked Havoc in Charleston," by Belvin Horres, *Charleston Evening Post*, September 25, 1958; and numerous articles from the *Charleston News and Courier*.

The author also interviewed Jack Leland, a Charleston journalist, several times and obtained information not contained in the books listed above.

Vengeance Is Mine

Among the sources consulted by the author were articles in newspapers, including the following: *The Sun News* (Myrtle Beach, South Carolina), March 28, 31, August 8, 9, 11, 12, 16, October 3, 15, 1978; March 26, April 10, 1979; March 29, 30, April 1, 2, 3, 4, October 10, 12, 1980; May 29, October 2, 3, 31, November 2, 3, 1986; *The State* (Columbia, South Carolina), August 10, 11, 15, 1978; March 15, 19, 25, 27, April 1, May 24, June 24, 25, 27, 29, 30, December 23, 29, 1983; September 12, 1984; January 23, April 11, 15, 21, 1985; March 20, 21, 22, 25, 26, July 28, 1986; and "The Seeds of Vengeance," by Art Harris, *The Washington Post*, June 24, 1983.

Background material on the Cimo family, and others involved in this story, was also obtained from the CBS feature movie *Vengeance: The Story of Tony Cimo.* Tony Cimo sold the film rights to the story to Nederlander Television and Film Productions of New York.

A Deadly Combination

Material in this story comes primarily from the following sources: *Winston-Salem Journal* (Winston-Salem, North Carolina), May 21, June 4, 1985; April 5, 1987; "Bitter Blood, A Genealogy of Murder," an eight-part series written by Jerry Bledsoe for the *Greensboro Daily News* (Greensboro, North Carolina), August 21-September 1, 1985; and "The Klenners and the Newsoms: Requiem for a Family," three serialized articles by William R. Trotter and Robert Newsom III, *Carolina Piedmont*, July/August, September, October, 1987.